MW01644651

ZOROASTRIANISM

Esoteric Teachings and the Priesthood of the Fire

Book #3

Esoteric Religious Studies Series
ZOROASTRIANISM
ESOTERIC TEACHINGS AND THE PRIESTHOOD OF THE FIRE

Author: Diohka Aesden
Publisher: Cineris Multifacet
Publication Date: 2023
ISBN: 9798398717396 (Paperback)
9798398720006 (Hardcover)

For inquiries and permissions, please contact:
Cineris Multifacet
cinerismultifacet@gmail.com

Design and Typesetting:
Cineris Multifacet

Cover Design:
Cineris Multifacet

Manufactured in the United States of America

First Edition: 2023

ISBN-13: 9798398717396 (Paperback)
9798398720006 (Hardcover)

19 54 95

This page left intentionally blank.

OTHER BOOKS IN THIS SERIES

1. Hermeticism and Alchemy in Renaissance Europe
2. Gnosticism: Ancient Mystical Traditions, Sects & Texts
3. Zoroastrianism: Esoteric Teachings and the Priesthood of the Fire
4. Sufism: Persian Mystical Path of Islam
5. Daoist Immortality and Internal Alchemy
6. Theurgy and Neoplatonic Mysticism
7. Shamanism in Siberia: Animism and Nature Worship
8. African Traditional Religions and Spirituality
9. Druidism and Celtic Mysticism
10. Indigenous Australian Dreamtime, Songlines and Ancestral Beings
11. Jyotish: Vedic Astrology
12. Hellenistic Mystery Cults: Thessalian Witchcraft & Ancient Greek Magic
13. Kabbalah: Jewish Mystical Tradition
14. Shinto: Japanese Indigenous Religion
15. Native American Spirituality and Vision Quests
16. Mesoamerican Shamanism and Divination
17. Ancient Egyptian Rituals and Symbolism
18. Norse Mythology and Runes
19. Rastafarianism: Spirituality and Social Movement
20. Jainism: Ascetic Practices and Philosophy
21. Romuva: Baltic Paganism, Witchcraft, and Folklore Revival
22. Vodou: Haitian Creole Religion
23. Maori Spirituality and Creation Myths
24. Hawaiian Huna Healing and Spirituality
25. Theosophy: Blending Eastern and Western Esotericism
26. Tibetan Bon: Ancient Shamanistic Tradition
27. Yoruba Religion and Orisha Worship
28. Esoteric Buddhism: Secret Teachings and Rituals
29. Romani Folklore and Mythology
30. Aztec Mythology and Cosmology
31. Bahá'í Faith: Unity of Religions
32. Hittite Religion and Rituals
33. Spiritualism: Communication with the Spirit World
34. Afro-Caribbean Syncretic Religions
35. Tantra: Ritual Practices and Symbolism
36. Armenian Folk Religion and Beliefs
37. Guarani Mythology and Cosmology
38. Esoteric Aspects of Islam: Batiniyya and Hurufism
39. Manichaeism: Dualistic Religion and Philosophy
40. Finnish Shamanism and Folk Magic
41. Ancient Sumerian Religion and Magic
42. Afro-Brazilian Umbanda and Candomblé
43. Tibetan Oracles and Divination Practices
44. Khoisan Spirituality: San Bushmen Traditions
45. Yezidi Religion: Angel Worship and the Sacred Peacock
46. Kalash Religion: Ancient Indo-Aryan Practices
47. Druze Esotericism: Secret Wisdom and Reincarnation
48. Burmese Nat Worship and Spirit Possession
49. Ancient Canaanite Religion: Rituals, Magical Texts and Spells
50. Etruscan Divination and Augury

51. Ainu Shamanism: Spiritual Practices in Northern Japan
52. Circassian Paganism and Ancestral Customs
53. Tengrism: Central Asian Shamanistic Beliefs
54. Mari El Paganism: Volga-Finnic Indigenous Religion
55. Haida Mythology and Totemism: Healing and Spirit Communication
56. Balinese Hindu-Buddhist Syncretism
57. Aramean Religion and Ancient Semitic Cults
58. Khoekhoen Religion: Southern African Indigenous Beliefs
59. Ojibwe Midewiwin: The Grand Medicine Society
60. Afro-Colombian Religions: Palenque and Santeria
61. Sámi Shamanism: Indigenous Spirituality of Northern Europe
62. Ossetian Folk Religion and Mythology
63. Mithraism: Ancient Mystery Cult of the Roman Empire
64. Ainu Bear Festival and Symbolism
65. Ancient Anatolia: Hittites and Luwians, and Lydian Goddess Cults
66. Toda Shamanism: Indigenous People of South India
67. Mesopotamian Magic and Incantations
68. Mande Paganism: West African Traditional Religions
69. Javanese Kejawen: Mystical Teachings and Rituals
70. Thracian Myth and Greco-Roman Orphic and Dionysian Mysteries
71. Maronite Christianity: Esoteric Practices and Traditions
72. Basque Mythology, Folklore, and Witchcraft
73. Gagauz Folk Religion and Rituals
74. Tagalog Mythology: Anito Spirits and Mythical Creatures
75. Hurrian Religion: Ancient Near Eastern Pantheon
76. Buryat Buddhism: Shamanistic Elements in Tibetan Buddhism
77. Selk'nam Cosmology and Ceremonies
78. Baka Pygmy Spirituality: Central African Indigenous Beliefs
79. Kumyk Paganism: Turkic Indigenous Religion
80. Scythian Religion and Warrior Culture
81. Venda Mythology: Sacred Lake and Rainmaker Rituals
82. Onondaga Longhouse Religion: Iroquois Spiritual Practices
83. Ewe-Fon Voodoo: West African Spiritual Practices
84. Manchu Shamanism: Indigenous Spirituality of Northeast Asia
85. Taíno Religion: Indigenous Beliefs of the Caribbean
86. Ancient Moabite Religion: Worship of Chemosh and Ashtaroth
87. Gallo-Roman Religion: Celtic Influence in Roman Gaul
88. Tsimshian Mythology: Stories of Raven and Trickster Figures
89. Manobo Indigenous Spirituality: Mindanao Tribal Beliefs
90. Pawnee Sacred Bundles and Tribal Ceremonies
91. Batak Shamanism: Indigenous Practices of North Sumatra
92. Breton Folklore: Legends and Supernatural Beings
93. Jivaroan Shamanism: Indigenous Traditions of the Amazon Rainforest
94. Alawite Mystical Teachings and Secret Practices
95. Silesian Folk Religion and Folklore
96. Igbo Odinani: Traditional Religion of the Igbo People
97. Rarámuri Shamanism: Indigenous Spirituality of the Tarahumara
98. Kikuyu Traditional Religion: Sacred Sites and Ancestor Worship
99. Ancient Numidian Religion: North African Indigenous Beliefs
100. Lurs Folk Religion and Rituals

A World of Esoteric Thought

Esoteric Religious Studies Series

ZOROASTRIANISM

Esoteric Teachings and the Priesthood of the Fire

Dedicated to

The Amesha Spentas

and to

Pope Philo III

ALPHA

May the reader of the Esoteric Religious Studies Series be blessed abundantly. We extend our heartfelt gratitude for your engagement with this sagacious study of esoteric traditions. As you adventure through the pages, may your mind be illuminated with knowledge and your heart be filled with wisdom. May the insights and revelations within these texts expand your understanding and bring clarity to your spiritual path. May you be well-informed, enriched, and guided by the sacred wisdom that unfolds before you. May this series be a source of inspiration, transformation, and blessings upon your life.

If you enjoy the words of this book, please consider leaving a review in the marketplace you found it so that its content can reach even more interested individuals.

TABLE OF CONTENTS

A

Ω

Part 1: Eloquence of Silence

ESOTERIC RELIGIOUS STUDIES SERIES

INTRODUCTION TO ELOQUENCE OF SILENCE

In the annals of world religion, few faiths are as storied, yet as seldom understood, as Zoroastrianism. "Zoroastrianism: Esoteric Teachings and the Priesthood of the Fire" journeys into the depths of this ancient tradition, examining its origins, exploring its teachings, and illuminating its profound influence on spiritual thought and practice. This work provides a study into a belief system that has persisted for millennia, its flame still flickering against the vast backdrop of spiritual beliefs across the globe.

The premise of Zoroastrianism traces back to Zarathustra, or Zoroaster, a prophet whose historical existence is much like the shadows cast by the sacred fire of the faith – dancing on the edge of reality and mystery. Yet, his teachings, immortalized within the 17 hymns of the *Gathas*, provide a fascinating glimpse into the heart of Zoroastrian philosophy. This book aims to dissect these verses, offering readers a chance to understand the poetic language of Zoroaster and the profound wisdom it imparts.

The text dives into a fundamental element of Zoroastrian belief: the cosmic struggle between *Ahura Mazda*, the embodiment of truth and goodness, and *Angra Mainyu*, the manifestation of deceit and evil. It explores how this battle, etched in the metaphysical plane, resonates through the physical world and the human psyche, shaping the journey of each individual soul.

Through an examination of Zoroastrian scriptures, including the *Avesta* and the *Gathas*, as well as the Revayats and Nasks, this book unveils the rich atlas of religious rites, moral codes, and esoteric teachings encapsulated within these texts. A study of key symbols, such as the holy fire and Towers of Silence, further helps decode Zoroastrian cosmology and theology, shedding light on how they reflect in the faith's rituals and ethics.

Zoroastrianism, in its essence, is not merely a religion of scriptures and rituals but a philosophy of life. Its core tenets,

Humata (good thoughts), *Hukhta* (good words), and *Hvarshta* (good deeds), offer profound insight into Zoroastrian ethics and its focus on leading a life of virtue. By discussing these principles in detail, this book highlights the religion's relevance in the contemporary world and its influence on the philosophies that succeeded it.

"Zoroastrianism: Esoteric Teachings and the Priesthood of the Fire" offers readers a comprehensive and detailed account of this ancient faith, capturing its essence and intricacies. Whether you are a spiritual seeker, a student of comparative religions, or merely intrigued by the world's oldest monotheistic religion, this book will serve as an invaluable guide to understanding Zoroastrianism and its lasting legacy.

I: ZOROASTRIANISM/MAZDAYASNA: THE DAWN OF MONOTHEISM

The sun rises over the barren lands of ancient Persia, its first rays awakening the land's innate vibrancy. Amidst this landscape, an equally potent awakening transpires – the birth of a faith that would influence the atlas of world religions in unprecedented ways. This is Zoroastrianism, also known as *Mazdayasna*, a beacon of monotheistic thought amidst the polytheistic societies of the time.

The inception of Zoroastrianism is intertwined with the story of its prophet, Zoroaster, or as the Greeks called him, Zarathustra. Historical accounts paint an unclear picture of

Zoroaster's existence, with proposed dates ranging from the 18th century BCE to the 6th century BCE. However, the uncertainty surrounding his life doesn't dim the luminosity of his teachings that form the core of Zoroastrian belief.

Zoroaster was reportedly a priest who, disillusioned with the prevalent religious practices of his time, sought solace in solitude. During one such retreat, he experienced a divine vision of *Vohu Manah* ("Good Purpose") that led him to *Ahura Mazda,* the "Wise Lord". This encounter marked the inception of Zoroastrianism, with *Ahura Mazda* emerging as the uncreated God, the supreme entity embodying truth and righteousness, and the one worthy of worship.

Zoroaster's revolutionary teachings didn't just challenge the existing religious order but also the social norms of the time. He advocated for the equality of all beings, irrespective of their class or gender, earning him both ardent followers and vehement opposition.

His teachings, immortalized in the holy *Gathas*, form the bedrock of the Zoroastrian faith. Written in an archaic form of the Avestan language, these 17 hymns are attributed directly to Zoroaster, offering insights into his philosophical and theological ideals. They depict a cosmic battle between truth (*Asha*) and deceit (*Druj*), a conflict between the forces of good and evil that transcends the metaphysical realm to influence human morality and behavior.

The *Gathas,* along with the rest of the *Avesta,* create a comprehensive religious scripture that delineates the nuances of Zoroastrian faith. The *Yasna,* for instance, consists of the liturgical texts used in ritual ceremonies, while the *Visperad* is dedicated to the ritual invocations of the divine entities. The *Vendidad,* on the other hand, provides a detailed account of Zoroastrian law, moral codes, and purification rituals.

Despite the numerous invasions, migrations, and cultural shifts that transpired over the centuries, Zoroastrianism managed to keep its flame alive, proving the resilience of its core beliefs. The faith's influence extends beyond the confines of its community, influencing major world religions, including Judaism, Christianity, and Islam, and continues to play a significant role in the cultural and religious landscape of Iran and India, the two countries with the largest Zoroastrian populations today.

By delving into the roots of Zoroastrianism, this chapter attempts to create a solid foundation for understanding its complexities. As we navigate through the subsequent chapters, we will explore the various aspects of this faith, its teachings, practices, and its long-lasting impact on the world.

II: Zoroaster: The Poet-Priest and Prophet of Ancient Persia

Zoroaster – the man, the prophet, the legend. His birth and life steeped in the fog of antiquity, Zoroaster emerges as a figure of monumental significance in the world's spiritual history. Known by many names - Zarathustra in Avestan, Zartosht in Persian, and Zoroaster in Greek - this prophet's teachings heralded a new dawn in the spiritual realm, kindling the light of Zoroastrianism.

In the historical records, Zoroaster is a figure shrouded in mystery. Scholars have struggled to agree on even his timeline, with proposed dates spanning centuries. While some argue that Zoroaster might have lived around 1200-1500 BCE, others propose later dates of around 600-500 BCE. Nonetheless, it is widely accepted that Zoroaster hailed from the Eastern part of the Iranian Plateau, an assertion substantiated by the linguistic characteristics of the *Gathas* and the geographical references in the *Avesta*.

While the details of Zoroaster's life might be elusive, his spiritual and philosophical contributions remain lucid. Born into a Bronze Age culture steeped in polytheistic traditions, Zoroaster was reportedly a priest. However, he soon grew disenchanted with the prevalent faith, which revolved around appeasing a pantheon of deities, many with capricious and wrathful dispositions.

His spiritual wanderings and meditations culminated in a series of revelations that dramatically shifted his worldview. In his visions, he encountered *Vohu Manah* (Good Purpose), leading him to the supreme entity - *Ahura Mazda*, the Wise Lord. Zoroaster's experiences formed the theological bedrock of Zoroastrianism, introducing monotheism amidst the prevailing polytheism of the time.

This revelation prompted Zoroaster to abandon the old gods – the *Daevas* – who were dethroned from divinity due to their preoccupation with war and conflict. Zoroaster's theology pivoted around *Ahura Mazda*, a benevolent deity embodying truth (*Asha*), righteousness, and wisdom. *Ahura Mazda* was uncreated, eternal, and omniscient, overseeing the cosmic order while respecting humanity's free will.

Zoroaster's teachings were revolutionary, not just in terms of theology but also in their sociopolitical implications. He eschewed the rigid social hierarchy of his time, promoting a merit-based society where individuals were valued for their righteousness. This stood in stark contrast to the prevalent class distinctions based on birth and profession, making Zoroaster's teachings appealing to the common populace while simultaneously attracting the ire of the elites.

Despite facing persecution and opposition, Zoroaster remained undeterred. His life's mission was to spread the message of *Ahura Mazda,* instilling the principles of Good Thoughts (*Humata*), Good Words (*Hukhta*), and Good Deeds (*Hvarshta*) into the societal fabric. These tenets emphasized individual responsibility in maintaining cosmic order, by choosing the path of truth and righteousness.

Zoroaster's spiritual legacy continues to reverberate through the millennia, embedded within the hymns of the *Gathas* and the rituals of Zoroastrianism. His image – that of a bearded man wearing a robe and holding a staff – is not merely an icon of a bygone era, but a symbol of a persistent faith and a testament to the indomitable human spirit in its quest for spiritual enlightenment.

In the next chapter, we will continue to explore Zoroastrianism, diving deeper into the teachings of Zoroaster, the divine entities, and the moral codes that constitute this ancient faith.

III: VOHU MANAH AND THE COSMIC BATTLE BETWEEN GOOD AND EVIL

Vohu Manah, loosely translated as "Good Purpose" or "Good Mind," stands as one of the pivotal concepts in Zoroastrianism. It represents the benevolent principle of wisdom and intelligence and is considered one of the seven *Amesha Spentas* or "Bounteous Immortals" in the Zoroastrian hierarchy of divinity. In Zoroaster's vision, *Vohu Manah* was the divine entity that led him to the supreme god, *Ahura Mazda.*

The concept of *Vohu Manah* isn't merely confined to a divine entity. It permeates into the daily life of Zoroastrians, where it embodies the wisdom needed to discern truth (*Asha*) from falsehood (*Druj*). This discernment forms the crux of the moral responsibility that each Zoroastrian is expected to uphold.

Zoroaster's theology provides an intriguing perspective on good and evil, personified as *Ahura Mazda* (the embodiment of good) and *Angra Mainyu* (the embodiment of evil). According to Zoroastrian belief, these two forces were uncreated, co-existing in a state of conflict at the beginning of creation.

Zoroaster preached that humans were free to choose between these two forces. Choosing *Ahura Mazda*'s path would lead them toward truth, righteousness, and an existence imbued with *Vohu Manah*. In contrast, following *Angra Mainyu* would take them toward deceit and chaos. Zoroaster's teachings were clear: while the existence of evil was acknowledged, the duty of every individual was to actively resist it and choose the path of righteousness.

This cosmic dichotomy, the clash between the forces of *Asha* and *Druj*, extends into a broader moral context. It mandates that every Zoroastrian should strive to cultivate Good Thoughts (*Humata*), Good Words (*Hukhta*), and Good Deeds (*Hvarshta*) as they navigate through their lives. These principles, symbolically represented as the threefold path of Zoroastrianism, form the moral compass guiding their ethical and spiritual choices.

Zoroastrianism, therefore, is not just a religion of rituals and hymns. It presents a comprehensive moral code intertwined with divine principles. It charges each individual with the responsibility of maintaining cosmic harmony by resisting falsehood and promoting truth.

In essence, *Vohu Manah* and the cosmic battle between good and evil lay the foundations for Zoroastrian ethics and morality. They chart a complex atlas where the spiritual and the ethical dimensions intersect, creating a faith that advocates individual responsibility, ethical living, and the persistent pursuit of truth.

In the subsequent chapters, we will continue to dive into the nuances of Zoroastrianism, exploring its scriptures, practices, and enduring influence.

In the next chapter, we will turn to one of the most sacred rituals in Zoroastrianism: the *Yasna*. This liturgical ceremony not only reflects the Zoroastrian worldview but also offers insights into the role of ritual and symbolism in this ancient faith.

IV: Yasna: The Sacred Rituals and Their Symbolism

The *Yasna,* one of Zoroastrianism's central liturgical rituals, stands as a testament to the faith's profound devotion to the divine. Its name derived from the Avestan word *yazi,* meaning "to sacrifice" or "to worship," the *Yasna* ceremony encapsulates the core principles and beliefs of the Zoroastrian faith, providing a fascinating window into its religious culture and practices.

The *Yasna* ritual, typically conducted by two priests, is a complex ceremony that revolves around the preparation and consecration of the *Haoma* plant and the holy drink derived from it. It also involves the offering of animal milk, fruits, and twigs of the pomegranate tree to the fire, which represents *Ahura Mazda*'s divine presence. The complexity of the *Yasna* ceremony is indicative of the detailed nature of Zoroastrian rituals and their symbolic value.

In the midst of the ritual, the priests chant verses from the *Yasna* text, which comprises 72 chapters and includes the sacred *Gathas*. The recitations are performed in an ancient liturgical language known as Avestan, which has largely fallen out of daily use but remains preserved within these religious contexts.

The *Haoma* plant, central to the *Yasna* ritual, holds a significant symbolic role. In Zoroastrian mythology, this sacred plant is associated with rejuvenation and enlightenment, and the act of pressing it during the *Yasna* ceremony signifies the extraction of its divine essence. Similarly, the ritualistic offerings to the sacred fire are symbolic gestures of piety, underscoring the Zoroastrians' reverence for nature's elements.

Yet, the *Yasna* ceremony is not merely a ritualistic practice; it encapsulates the Zoroastrian cosmic drama. The consecration of the *Haoma,* the invocation of the divine entities, and the ritual offerings to the sacred fire, all embody the eternal battle between the forces of good and evil. By participating in the *Yasna,* Zoroastrians engage in this cosmic battle, reaffirming their commitment to *Ahura Mazda* and the path of *Asha*.

The *Yasna* ritual, thus, offers a microcosm of the Zoroastrian worldview, with its emphasis on ritual purity, moral responsibility, and devotion to *Ahura Mazda*. It stands as a bridge between the human and divine realms, an affirmation of faith, and a testament to Zoroastrianism's enduring spiritual legacy.

As we move into the following chapters, we will dive deeper into Zoroastrianism's holy texts, its priesthood, and its enduring influence in shaping the spiritual and cultural landscape of various civilizations.

In the next chapter, we will explore the *Avesta*, the primary collection of sacred texts in Zoroastrianism, and its profound theological insights.

V: THE AVESTA: THE HOLY TEXTS OF ZOROASTRIANISM

The *Avesta,* often regarded as the Bible of Zoroastrianism, serves as the primary collection of sacred texts that have guided the faith's followers over millennia. It's a compilation of different texts composed over several centuries and contains hymns, liturgies, and theological and philosophical teachings. Through its profound verses, the *Avesta* provides insights into the Zoroastrian worldview and moral code.

The *Avesta* can be divided into two main sections: the *Yasna* and the *Vendidad.* The *Yasna,* which includes the *Gathas,* comprises hymns and liturgical texts used in rituals and ceremonies, like the *Yasna* ceremony discussed in the previous chapter. The *Gathas,* attributed directly to Zoroaster, are at the heart of Zoroastrian theology. Composed in an ancient form of Avestan language, these 17 hymns encapsulate the prophet's revelations and teachings.

The *Vendidad,* on the other hand, is a legal and mythological text, containing directives on various matters such as purification rituals and societal laws. It also narrates myths, including the story of creation and the first man, providing an understanding of Zoroastrian cosmogony and anthropology.

Alongside these two main sections, the *Avesta* includes the *Visperad,* a liturgical extension of the *Yasna,* and the *Yashts,* hymns dedicated to individual deities or spiritual beings. The *Khorda Avesta,* or '*Little Avesta,*' contains shorter prayers for everyday use by ordinary Zoroastrians.

These texts have been faithfully transmitted from generation to generation, first orally and then written down in the Middle Persian script around the 5th century CE. Even today, they are recited in their original form during Zoroastrian rituals and ceremonies, serving as a bridge to the faith's ancient past.

However, the *Avesta*'s significance extends beyond its role as a liturgical text. It encapsulates the Zoroastrian ethical triad of Good Thoughts, Good Words, and Good Deeds. It instills in its followers a profound respect for the natural world, emphasizing purity and cleanliness. And above all, it reiterates the cosmic conflict between good and evil, urging individuals to choose righteousness.

The *Avesta*, therefore, serves not only as a spiritual guide but also as a moral compass for Zoroastrians. Its verses illuminate the path of righteousness, urging its followers to lead a life in harmony with nature and the divine, thus sustaining the cosmic order.

In the upcoming chapters, we will further examine the role of priesthood in Zoroastrianism, the significance of fire temples, and the impact of Zoroastrianism on global religious and philosophical systems. In the next chapter, we will dive into the complex structure of the Zoroastrian priesthood and its crucial role in preserving and propagating the faith.

VI: THE ZOROASTRIAN PRIESTHOOD: KEEPERS OF THE FLAME

The Zoroastrian faith assigns a pivotal role to its priesthood, responsible for maintaining the faith's traditions, conducting religious rituals, and serving as spiritual guides for the community. Known collectively as the *Mobeds*, these priests have, for centuries, acted as the custodians of Zoroastrian teachings and practices.

The journey to becoming a *Mobed* begins early, often during childhood, and involves a comprehensive understanding of Zoroastrian rituals, ethics, and ancient languages. It is a path of profound dedication, requiring the aspirant to embody the principles of Good Thoughts, Good Words, and Good Deeds in their daily life.

The Zoroastrian priesthood comprises different levels, starting with the *Ervads,* who conduct basic ceremonies, followed by *Mobeds* who perform more complex rituals. At the apex are the *Dasturs,* the high priests, revered as learned scholars and leaders within the Zoroastrian community. They are consulted on matters of religious law and spiritual guidance and often act as the community's representatives in the wider world.

The priest's role is not confined to religious observance but extends to education, guidance, and community service. Zoroastrian priests are tasked with preserving the teachings of the *Avesta,* instructing the younger generation, and leading community efforts in maintaining the purity of the elements, a vital aspect of Zoroastrian practice.

The priesthood's integral part in Zoroastrianism is symbolically represented in the *Atash Bahram,* or "Victorious Fire," the highest grade of fire in the Zoroastrian religion, housed in the fire temples. The fire, meticulously consecrated in a complex ritual involving 16 different sources, is considered a living embodiment of *Ahura Mazda*'s wisdom. It's the responsibility of the priests to maintain this sacred fire, which has to be kept burning continuously.

In this role, the Zoroastrian priests are aptly referred to as "Keepers of the Flame," preserving not only the sacred fire but the spiritual flame of Zoroastrianism itself. Despite their numbers dwindling over the years, these priests continue to hold the fort, ensuring that the teachings and practices of one of the world's oldest religions continue to thrive.

In the chapters to follow, we will investigate Zoroastrian sacred sites, dive into the faith's cosmology, and explore its influences on other religious traditions. The next chapter will take us to the magnificent *Fire Temple of Yazd*, a testament to the Zoroastrians' reverence for the divine element of fire.

VII: Fire Temple of Yazd: a Beacon of Zoroastrian Faith

The *Fire Temple of Yazd,* located in Iran, is a remarkable emblem of Zoroastrianism's spiritual and architectural heritage. It's an embodiment of the religion's elemental worship, particularly of fire, which Zoroastrians perceive as a symbol of *Ahura Mazda*'s divine wisdom and purity.

Built in 1934, the temple houses an *Atash Bahram,* or "Victorious Fire," the highest grade of consecrated fire in Zoroastrianism. This sacred fire, kept in a bronze urn behind a glass screen, has been burning continuously since 470 AD, tended by the temple's priests who ensure that the flame never extinguishes.

The temple's architecture pays homage to the principles of Zoroastrianism. At the temple's entrance, one is greeted by a *Fravahar*, the iconic winged symbol of Zoroastrianism, symbolizing the human soul's journey towards perfection. The temple complex also includes a garden and a small pool, further embodying the Zoroastrian reverence for nature and its elements.

The *Fire Temple of Yazd* is not merely a place of worship but also a symbol of cultural resilience. Despite centuries of religious and political upheaval, the Yazd temple stands as a testament to the enduring legacy of Zoroastrian faith and practice.

Its sacred flame, an enduring beacon of light, mirrors the undying spirit of Zoroastrianism. Each flicker tells a tale of a civilization's rise and fall, of religious persecution, of cultural assimilation, and above all, of unyielding faith. It is a testament to the commitment of Zoroastrian priests and communities who have worked tirelessly to keep the fire burning, literally and metaphorically.

In the heart of Iran, a country predominantly Islamic, the *Fire Temple of Yazd* serves as a precious reminder of the country's pre-Islamic past and cultural plurality. It remains a pilgrimage site for Zoroastrians worldwide, drawing seekers and scholars intrigued by the ancient religion.

As we move forward in this study, we will further dive into Zoroastrian teachings, such as the concept of dualism and the importance of moral choice. We'll also touch upon the role Zoroastrianism has played in shaping other world religions, and its contemporary practices. The next chapter dives into one of the most profound and contested elements of Zoroastrianism: the doctrine of dualism.

VIII: DUALISM IN ZOROASTRIANISM: ANGRA MAINYU AND SPENTA MAINYU

Inherent to Zoroastrian thought is the concept of dualism, reflected in the cosmic struggle between good and evil, embodied by *Ahura Mazda*'s twin spirits: *Spenta Mainyu,* the "Bountiful Spirit," and *Angra Mainyu,* the "Destructive Spirit."

Spenta Mainyu and *Angra Mainyu* are opposing entities. *Spenta Mainyu* represents the principles of truth, light, life, and beneficence, facilitating creation and existence. In contrast, *Angra Mainyu* is a manifestation of deceit, darkness, destruction, and malevolence, intent on sowing chaos and obstructing life's thriving harmony.

These two forces are not mere abstract concepts but active agents influencing the physical and moral world. They represent the choices available to every individual, between righteous actions aligned with *Ahura Mazda,* and harmful deeds assisting the Destructive Spirit. The tension between these opposing forces underlies the Zoroastrian emphasis on moral choice, a central tenet in its teachings.

Yet, Zoroastrian dualism is not absolute. *Ahura Mazda,* the "Wise Lord," stands supreme, the source of both spirits, making Zoroastrianism essentially monotheistic. The two spirits are unevenly matched, and the outcome of their struggle is predetermined. Zoroastrian scriptures prophesy a time when good will finally vanquish evil, establishing a state of perfection on earth, referred to as the *Frashokereti,* the subject of a later chapter.

In this light, Zoroastrianism encourages its followers to align with the Bountiful Spirit, urging them to uphold truth and righteousness in thoughts, words, and deeds, thus participating in the cosmic battle against deceit and discord. It fosters an ethical lifestyle aimed at promoting good and combating evil in everyday life, enabling individuals to contribute to the realization of the *Frashokereti.*

This nuanced understanding of dualism reflects Zoroastrianism's moral and philosophical depth, influencing other religious traditions in significant ways. In the chapters ahead, we'll continue exploring Zoroastrian beliefs, practices, and their impacts, delving next into the lesser-known entities of Zoroastrian cosmology: *Aka Manah* and *Ahriman*.

IX: THE DESTRUCTIVE FORCES: AKA MANAH AND AHRIMAN

In Zoroastrianism's moral universe, the forces of deceit and chaos are personified by two key figures: *Aka Manah* and *Ahriman.* Their roles in the religious narrative shed further light on the Zoroastrian concept of dualism and moral choice.

Aka Manah, whose name translates to "Evil Mind" or "Evil Purpose," is often viewed as the chief lieutenant of *Angra Mainyu,* the Destructive Spirit. *Aka Manah* embodies falsehood and deception, standing in direct opposition to *Vohu Manah,* the "Good Mind." He represents the temptation to choose ill-thought actions over wise and benevolent ones, thus creating discord in the cosmic order.

In Zoroastrian texts, *Aka Manah* is often depicted attempting to lead individuals astray, coaxing them to abandon the path of righteousness. His antagonism isn't just limited to mankind; even Zoroaster himself was a target of *Aka Manah*'s attempts to divert him from his divine mission, as outlined in the *Gathas*.

Ahriman (a Middle Persian form of *Angra Mainyu*) is another crucial figure in Zoroastrianism, representing the cosmic force of destruction and evil. While *Angra Mainyu* is the original Avestan term, the name *Ahriman* gained prominence in later Zoroastrian texts, notably in the *Bundahishn*, a Zoroastrian account of creation.

Ahriman is depicted as an adversary to *Ahura Mazda*, spreading chaos and suffering in the world. However, it's important to note that he is not considered an equal and independent force to *Ahura Mazda*. In Zoroastrian theology, *Ahriman* is a fallen aspect of the divine creation, a misguided spirit whose ultimate defeat is assured.

Aka Manah and *Ahriman* play pivotal roles in the Zoroastrian narrative, personifying the choices faced by humanity in its quest for spiritual growth. The struggle against these destructive forces symbolizes the ethical journey every

Zoroastrian is encouraged to undertake, aligning with the path of truth, righteousness, and benevolence.

In the next chapter, we'll dive deeper into Zoroastrian cosmology, exploring the spiritual realms of *Getig* and *Menog*, and their significance in Zoroastrian theology.

X: Zoroastrian Cosmology: The Realms of Getig and Menog

Zoroastrianism presents a fascinating cosmological vision encompassing two parallel realms: *Getig* and *Menog*. These realms represent the physical and spiritual dimensions of existence, respectively.

Getig, or *Gaētī* in Avestan, signifies the material world, the earthly plane where humans reside. It's a realm of form, of physicality, where life unfolds in a temporal sequence. The trials and tribulations encountered in this realm are viewed as opportunities for the soul's growth and maturation, fostering the cultivation of good thoughts, good words, and good deeds.

In contrast, *Menog*, or *Mēnōg*, signifies the spiritual world, the realm of thoughts, emotions, and the soul. It's believed to be timeless, unaffected by the physical laws governing the *Getig*. In the *Menog* realm, spiritual entities such as *Ahura Mazda*, the *Amesha Spentas*, and other divine beings reside.

In Zoroastrianism, life is viewed as a journey across these realms. The soul is believed to originate in the *Menog* realm, descends into the *Getig* to experience life, and upon death, returns to the spiritual realm. This return is not viewed as a final destination but as a stage in the soul's evolutionary journey. Depending on the soul's deeds during its earthly life, it either progresses towards the divine or undergoes purification before its onward journey.

The *Fravashi*, a person's divine guardian spirit, facilitates this journey across realms. The *Fravashi* is believed to remain in the *Menog* realm while guiding and protecting the soul in the *Getig*.

In this framework, the realms of *Getig* and *Menog* symbolize the interplay between the seen and the unseen, the temporal and the timeless, the physical and the spiritual. Such an understanding encourages Zoroastrians to view life holistically, recognizing their responsibility towards both the material and spiritual aspects of existence.

As we dive deeper into Zoroastrian cosmology, we'll explore the divine beings aiding the spiritual journey in the coming chapters, beginning with the powerful *Amesha Spentas*.

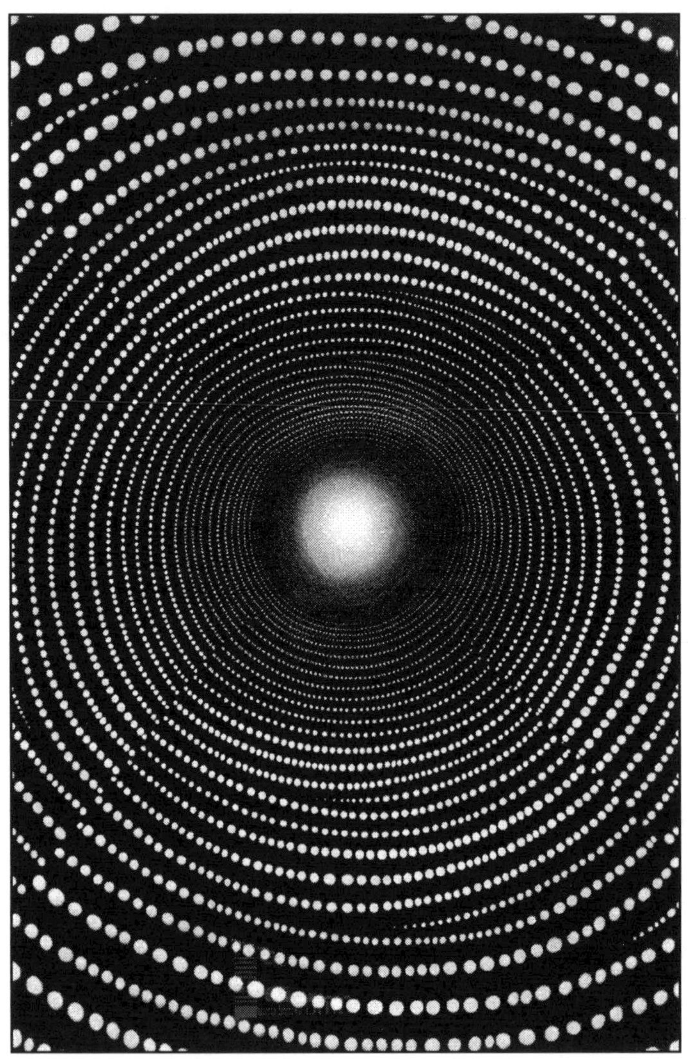

XI: THE AMESHA SPENTAS: SEVEN PILLARS OF EXISTENCE

In the grand atlas of Zoroastrian cosmology, the *Amesha Spentas* or "Bounteous Immortals" hold a pivotal place. These divine beings, created by *Ahura Mazda,* are manifestations of the divine attributes and serve as guides for humans to live righteously.

The seven *Amesha Spentas,* including *Ahura Mazda,* each correspond to an aspect of creation and a moral principle:

1. *Ahura Mazda* (Ohrmazd): The Wise Lord himself is considered the first *Amesha Spenta,* embodying wisdom and

enlightenment. He represents the entirety of existence and the source of all other *Amesha Spentas*.

2. *Vohu Manah* (*Vohuman*): Representing "Good Mind" or "Righteous Purpose," *Vohu Manah* encourages individuals to make morally sound choices. He is associated with animal creation, particularly beneficent animals like cattle.

3. *Asha Vahishta* (*Ardavahisht*): Meaning "Best Truth," *Asha Vahishta* embodies righteousness and cosmic order. He is associated with fire, symbolizing truth and transformation.

4. *Kshathra Vairya* (*Shahrewar*): Translating to "Desirable Dominion," this *Amesha Spenta* represents just leadership and social order. He governs the sky, representing the vast expanse of *Ahura Mazda*'s kingdom.

5. *Spenta Armaiti* (*Spandarmad*): Signifying "Devout Piety," *Spenta Armaiti* encourages devotion and benevolence towards all creations. She is linked to Mother Earth, emphasizing respect and stewardship for the planet.

6. *Haurvatat* (*Hordad*): Denoting "Wholeness," *Haurvatat* is the *Amesha Spenta* of health and prosperity. She presides over water, symbolizing life and purification.

7. *Ameretat* (*Amurdad*): Meaning "Immortality," *Ameretat* represents eternal life and the resilience of the spirit. She is associated with plant life, reinforcing the principle of growth and rejuvenity.

The *Amesha Spentas,* with their moral mandates and elemental associations, provide a framework for ethical living. They emphasize harmony with nature and moral integrity, encouraging Zoroastrians to embody these divine qualities in their daily life.

Having understood these divine forces, let's examine the Zoroastrian initiation ceremony, *Navjote,* and its significance in shaping a Zoroastrian's life journey, in the following chapter.

XII: Navjote: The Initiation into Zoroastrianism

Navjote is the initiation ceremony marking a young Zoroastrian's formal entrance into the faith. It is a rite of passage that reinforces the community's continuity, conferring upon the initiate the responsibilities of Zoroastrian moral and religious observances.

The ceremony typically takes place when a child reaches an age of understanding, often between seven and fifteen years. The exact age may vary, reflecting the belief that the individual should consciously accept the religion's principles. The ceremony's timing also draws from the ancient

Zoroastrian custom of vesting responsibility onto an individual after they reach the age of seven.

During the *Navjote,* the child is bathed in consecrated water, symbolizing purification. The child then dons the *sudreh,* a white cotton undershirt, and the *kusti,* a woolen thread girdle. The *sudreh,* representing righteousness, and the *kusti,* symbolizing the path of righteousness, become constant reminders of their religious obligations.

The highlight of the ceremony is when the child recites the '*Ahunavar,*' a sacred Zoroastrian prayer, in the presence of a priest and witnesses. By reciting this prayer, the child declares their allegiance to Zoroastrianism and commits to upholding its principles.

The *Navjote* ceremony serves not just as an initiation but as a reaffirmation of the community's values. It symbolizes the continuation of Zoroastrian teachings and the community's commitment to sustaining its religious and ethical heritage.

With the initiation complete, a Zoroastrian begins their journey in the faith, guided by a series of spiritual guides and leaders, which we'll explore next with a look into the Zoroastrian religious hierarchy: *Osta, Osti, Ervad* (*Hirbod*), *Mobed,* and *Dastur.*

XIII: Zoroastrian Hierarchy: Osta, Osti, Ervad, Mobed, and Dastur

Zoroastrianism is not only about individual practice but also maintains a structured religious hierarchy to preside over religious rituals and provide spiritual guidance to its community.

1. *Osta* and *Osti*: The basic unit of the Zoroastrian community is the family. The terms *Osta* (for men) and *Osti* (for women) are often used as respectful forms of address for laypeople, particularly older individuals. While not formally ordained, they play a crucial role in preserving Zoroastrian values and traditions within the family and community.

2. *Ervad* or *Hirbod*: This is the first level of ordained priesthood in Zoroastrianism. An *Ervad* has undergone the *Navar* ceremony, a religious initiation that permits him to perform simple religious rituals. However, he can't preside over higher-level ceremonies.

3. *Mobed*: A *Mobed* is a higher-level priest who has undergone both the *Navar* and the *Maratab* initiations. This level of priesthood permits him to preside over all regular rituals and ceremonies, except those reserved for the *Dasturs*.

4. *Dastur*: The *Dastur* is the highest rank in the Zoroastrian priesthood. A *Dastur* is not only well-versed in religious texts and laws but also possesses the spiritual authority to make interpretative decisions on religious matters. *Dasturs* preside over the most significant and sacred ceremonies, such as the consecration of a new fire temple.

This hierarchical structure helps ensure the continuity and integrity of Zoroastrian religious practice, providing the community with guidance and maintaining the sanctity of rituals. Despite the hierarchical nature, Zoroastrianism emphasizes that every individual, regardless of their position, has a role in sustaining the faith and its principles.

After this study of the human facilitators of the faith, we will return to the divine and spiritual, with a focus on *Aban* and *Atar*, the Zoroastrian divinities of waters and fire, respectively.

XIV: ABAN AND ATAR: THE TWIN FLAMES OF WATER AND FIRE

In the pantheon of Zoroastrian divinities, *Aban* and *Atar,* signifying waters and fire respectively, hold special significance. Both elements carry deep symbolic meanings, representing the purifying forces in the Zoroastrian faith.

Aban, meaning "waters" in Avestan, embodies the element water's nourishing and life-giving aspects. The divinity, also known as *Aredvi Sura Anahita* in the Avestan scriptures, is often depicted as a beautiful maiden, flowing eternally, purifying all that she touches. The reverence towards *Aban* is not just for the physical entity of water, but for the spiritual properties it signifies: purity, fertility, and wisdom.

Water is regarded as a source of life in Zoroastrianism. It's viewed as a vital element that sustains life on earth. Rivers, seas, and rain are all manifestations of *Aban*, contributing to the cycle of life. It's no coincidence that many Zoroastrian rituals involve ablutions, emphasizing the purifying aspect of water.

Parallel to *Aban*, *Atar*, meaning "fire" in Avestan, represents another crucial aspect of Zoroastrianism. *Atar*, the divine fire, is not just the physical fire but symbolizes the divine spark within every creation. It's viewed as a symbol of truth, righteousness, and divine illumination.

Fire in Zoroastrianism is seen as a channel for communicating with *Ahura Mazda*. It's an eternal witness to human deeds, and thus the presence of fire is essential in all religious rituals. Fire temples, known as *Atash Behram*, house consecrated fires that are kept burning continuously, symbolizing the eternal presence of *Ahura Mazda*.

Yet, *Atar* is not just the external fire in the temples; it is also the internal fire, the divine spark that prompts individuals towards truth and righteousness. As such, every Zoroastrian is responsible for keeping this inner fire alive through their good thoughts, good words, and good deeds.

This twin reverence of *Aban* and *Atar* highlights the Zoroastrian belief in harmony between different elements of nature. It emphasizes the Zoroastrian principle of respecting and maintaining the purity of natural elements, each holding significant symbolism in the faith's spiritual framework.

In the next chapter, we will explore another significant institution of Zoroastrian faith, the *Priesthood of Fire*. The discussion will involve an in-depth understanding of how the Zoroastrian faith perceives fire not just as a natural element, but as a living embodiment of divinity.

XV: THE PRIESTHOOD OF FIRE: AN EVERLASTING COVENANT

Fire, or *Atar*, holds a distinctive place in Zoroastrianism. It is not only considered a sacred element but an entity which encapsulates divine essence, symbolizing *Ahura Mazda*'s light and wisdom. The *priesthood of fire* signifies an ancient tradition of tending, worshipping, and preserving the divine fire.

Zoroastrian priests, also known as *Athravans* or "tenders of the fire", shoulder the responsibility of maintaining the sacred fire in Fire Temples, or *Atash Behrams*. These fires are not ordinary flames; they are meticulously consecrated through a rigorous and elaborate process. The process involves collecting sixteen different types of fire, each from a different source, such as a potter's kiln, a goldsmith's fire, a baker's oven, a shepherd's house, and lightning, to name a few.

This unification of sixteen fires signifies the amalgamation of society's different strata, reflecting the Zoroastrian ethos of community harmony. The gathered fire undergoes a purification ritual that lasts for a year, purged with sulfur and sandalwood, and consecrated with prayers before it's considered an *Atash Behram,* a "victorious fire".

Priests ensure the fire is never extinguished, symbolizing the eternal presence of divinity. This responsibility also extends to protecting the fire from any defilement. Zoroastrians believe that no impure matter should sully the fire, reinforcing the faith's emphasis on purity.

The *Priesthood of Fire* is not merely a title or role; it's a lifelong commitment. It's an eternal covenant between the priest and the divine, wherein the priest pledges to safeguard the sacred fire, uphold the faith's teachings, and serve as a spiritual guide for the community.

The sacred fire serves as an eternal beacon of hope, guiding Zoroastrians towards righteousness. It's a constant reminder of their faith and the principles of good thoughts, good words, and good deeds. The fire's warmth signifies *Ahura*

Mazda's love, its light symbolizes divine wisdom, and its ceaseless burning represents the Zoroastrians' unwavering faith.

In the following chapter, we dive into one of the most distinctive architectural and cultural symbols of Zoroastrianism: the Towers of Silence or *Dakhma,* where the Zoroastrians perform their unique funerary rituals. While the practice has largely ceased in many parts of the world due to societal changes, it still represents a significant part of the Zoroastrian understanding of life, death, and purity.

XVI: TOWERS OF SILENCE: ECHOES OF ZOROASTRIAN FUNERARY PRACTICES

Among the many unique aspects of Zoroastrianism, one of the most distinctive is its approach to death and the rituals surrounding it. Zoroastrian funerary practices, particularly the use of *Dakhmas* or Towers of Silence, illustrate a profound respect for the elements of nature and an unwavering commitment to the preservation of their purity.

A Tower of Silence is essentially a circular, raised structure used for the exposure of the dead. According to Zoroastrian belief, death is not a natural occurrence but an assault on life by *Angra Mainyu,* the destructive spirit. The corpse, subjected to this assault, becomes a vessel of impurity and must not be allowed to defile the sacred elements of fire, water, or earth.

Consequently, traditional Zoroastrian funerary practice avoids cremation or burial. Instead, bodies are placed in Towers of Silence, exposed to the sun and carrion birds. This method, referred to as *excarnation*, ensures the swift and efficient disposal of the physical body without contaminating the sacred elements.

The architecture of the Towers of Silence is meticulously designed to facilitate this process. The inner surface of the tower is divided into concentric rings with shallow grooves, allowing for the segregation of bodies by gender and age. The central pit collects the bones once the flesh has been consumed, ensuring no contact with the earth.

Despite its starkly pragmatic approach, the Zoroastrian funerary tradition is underpinned by a deep sense of respect and ritual. The rites begin at the moment of death with the *Sagdid* ceremony, where a dog is brought in to look upon the deceased, a ritual believed to drive away evil spirits.

Following this, a priest performs the *Geh Sarna,* a prayer asking for the deceased's soul to reach the divine realm. The body, meanwhile, is thoroughly washed and dressed in clean white clothes. The family then transports the body to the

Tower of Silence, where the *Nas-Salars* (corpse bearers) take over.

While the body is consigned to the tower, the soul's journey continues. The *Chaharum* ceremony, held four days after death, marks the soul's crossing into the spiritual realm. It's a critical moment, with prayers said to aid the soul's ascension and protect it from demonic influences.

However, modern times have seen changes to these ancient practices. Legal restrictions and shifts in societal norms have led many Zoroastrians, particularly those in diaspora communities, to adopt cremation or burial. Yet, the core principle guiding these practices - the preservation of elemental purity - remains intact.

In a broader sense, the Zoroastrian funerary tradition is a reflection of the faith's wider ecological consciousness. This concern for preserving nature's sanctity is not merely a theological stance but an actively practiced component of their religious life.

In the next chapter, we'll explore another fundamental aspect of Zoroastrian community organization: the *Council of Tehran Mobeds*. This council, as a religious authority, plays a vital role in guiding the Zoroastrian community and preserving their religious and cultural heritage. Their influence extends to the interpretation of religious law, the training and ordination of priests, and the resolution of community disputes. As we shall see, their role is integral to the preservation and continuity of the Zoroastrian faith.

XVII: THE COUNCIL OF TEHRAN MOBEDS: GUARDIANS OF ZOROASTRIAN LEGACY

Zoroastrianism, as one of the world's oldest surviving religions, has faced its share of trials and tribulations over the centuries. Despite the significant challenges, the faith continues to persist, thanks in no small part to institutions like the *Council of Tehran Mobeds.*

In Zoroastrianism, *Mobeds* are priests who perform religious ceremonies. They are crucial figures within the community, serving as spiritual guides and carrying out essential rituals. The *Council of Tehran Mobeds,* or *Anjoman-e-Mobedan,* is a body that oversees these priests, providing guidance, resolving disputes, and ensuring the faith's tenets are upheld.

Founded in 1924 in Tehran, Iran, the Council represents the interests of Zoroastrian *Mobeds* in the capital city, which has the largest concentration of Zoroastrians in the country. The Council's work is multifaceted, ranging from educational to judicial tasks. They offer religious guidance to the community, help settle religious disputes, train future *Mobeds*, and undertake initiatives to preserve and promote Zoroastrianism.

The *Council of Tehran Mobeds* plays an essential role in maintaining the continuity of religious practices and preserving Zoroastrian traditions. They ensure the correct performance of rituals and ceremonies, upholding the faith's emphasis on good thoughts, good words, and good deeds.

Through its educational endeavors, the Council also ensures the transmission of Zoroastrian knowledge to future generations. They run religious classes, teaching children about Zoroastrian history, the significance of rituals, and the principles of the faith.

However, the Council's role extends beyond religious instruction. They also act as a unifying force for the community, providing a platform for Zoroastrians to come together and support each other. They organize cultural events and community gatherings, fostering a sense of unity and mutual support among Zoroastrians.

One of the most crucial responsibilities of the Council is its role in ordaining new *Mobeds*. The process is rigorous, with candidates undergoing intensive religious training and demonstrating a deep understanding of Zoroastrian scriptures and rituals.

Despite the Council's crucial role, it faces considerable challenges. With the global Zoroastrian population dwindling, there are fewer candidates coming forward to become *Mobeds*. Furthermore, Zoroastrians living in diaspora often struggle to maintain their religious practices and connections with their ancestral faith.

Despite these challenges, the *Council of Tehran Mobeds* remains steadfast, working tirelessly to preserve and propagate Zoroastrianism. Through their dedication, they ensure the ancient fire of Zoroastrianism continues to burn brightly, guiding its followers towards truth and righteousness.

In the subsequent chapters, we shall dive into the concept of the *Sixteen Perfect Lands* and the potential historical interaction between Zoroastrianism and other cultures such as the Western Zhou dynasty. Each of these subjects offer compelling insights into the extensive influence of Zoroastrian thought and its impact on various civilizations.

XVIII: THE SIXTEEN PERFECT LANDS: AHURA MAZDA'S CREATION

The idea of the *Sixteen Perfect Lands,* or *Khvaniratha,* offers profound insights into Zoroastrian cosmology. According to Zoroastrian belief, *Ahura Mazda* created these lands as ideal habitats for humanity, each epitomizing harmony, prosperity, and purity. However, these lands were not spared from the assault of *Angra Mainyu,* the destructive spirit, who disrupted their perfection with adversity, underscoring the faith's dualistic nature.

The concept of the *Sixteen Lands* is mentioned in the *Vendidad,* one of the main texts in the *Avesta,* the holy book of

Zoroastrianism. While the text doesn't detail the specific location of these lands, they're portrayed as diverse, each possessing unique geographical and climatic characteristics. One land is described as flat and windy, another as mountainous, while another suffers from severe winters.

The *Sixteen Perfect Lands* symbolize the full spectrum of Earth's diversity and the inherent challenges each terrain can present. In this, they also represent the challenges of life and human resilience to adapt, survive, and thrive, despite adversity. As humans cultivate these lands, face their unique hardships and overcome them, they uphold the Zoroastrian principle of good conquering evil, of *Asha* overcoming *Druj*.

The *Sixteen Lands* also offer a metaphorical representation of the journey of the soul. Each land, with its unique challenges and hardships, can be viewed as stages in the soul's journey towards perfection, mirroring the human quest for spiritual growth and enlightenment.

Moreover, this concept has informed Zoroastrian ethics and ecology. The stewardship of the earth is a crucial duty for Zoroastrians, seen as part of their struggle against evil. They consider environmental degradation a form of *Druj*, to be combatted with practices that promote sustainability and respect for nature.

In the next chapter, we'll take a closer look at Zoroastrianism's interaction with other cultures, specifically during the Western Zhou Dynasty. The exchange of ideas between these two ancient cultures offers a fascinating study of the cross-cultural dissemination and convergence of spiritual beliefs and practices.

Despite the geographical distance and differences in language and culture, the ideological interactions between Zoroastrianism and ancient Chinese beliefs provide a compelling testimony to the enduring and far-reaching influence of Zoroastrian thought. By tracing these historical connections, we can gain a better understanding of the expansive spiritual landscape of the ancient world.

XIX: ZOROASTRIAN INFLUENCE ON THE WESTERN ZHOU DYNASTY

Ancient civilizations did not exist in isolation; cultural exchanges were common and often left lasting impacts. An example of this exchange is the potential influence of Zoroastrian thought on the philosophies that arose during the Western Zhou Dynasty in China.

Established around the 11th century BCE, the Western Zhou Dynasty marked a period of significant philosophical growth in ancient China. During this era, Zhou philosophers formulated concepts that later evolved into the foundations of Daoism, a significant spiritual tradition in Chinese history.

Simultaneously, Zoroastrianism was spreading westward from ancient Persia through trade routes. The question that arises here is whether these two philosophical traditions might have intersected, allowing Zoroastrian thought to influence the developing philosophical concepts in Zhou China.

This idea is supported by several parallels between Zoroastrian and Daoist beliefs. Both traditions emphasize living in harmony with nature, morality, and the cyclical nature of life and the universe. Zoroastrianism's emphasis on duality, particularly the struggle between good and evil, resembles Daoist notions of yin and yang. Also, the Zoroastrian reverence for the elements, particularly fire, echoes in Daoist rituals.

One of the significant areas of similarity is the concept of an ideal ruler. In Zoroastrianism, *Ahura Mazda* is portrayed as a benevolent deity guiding humans towards *Asha*, truth, and righteousness. In Zhou philosophy, the ruler was deemed the '*Son of Heaven*', a conduit between the divine and the human world, responsible for maintaining harmony and balance.

These parallels suggest a potential influence of Zoroastrian thought on Zhou philosophy. However, it's crucial to remember that such exchanges are rarely one-sided. If

Zoroastrian thought influenced Zhou philosophy, the reverse could also be true. It's also possible that these similarities arose independently in response to shared human experiences and needs, rather than through direct contact.

Despite these caveats, exploring the potential connections between Zoroastrianism and the philosophies of the Western Zhou Dynasty underscores the interconnectedness of human civilizations. Ideas, like people, traverse geographical boundaries, intertwining the fates and cultures of disparate societies. Our study of these connections continues in the following chapter, focusing on the intriguing parallels between Zoroastrianism and the Vedic religion.

XX: ZOROASTRIANISM AND THE VEDIC RELIGION: A CONVERGENCE OF FAITHS

Given their geographical proximity and shared Indo-Iranian roots, it's unsurprising that Zoroastrianism and the Vedic religion, the predecessor of modern Hinduism, share several similarities. While both religions evolved independently, their theological, ritualistic, and linguistic parallels suggest a common ancestry, indicating an intriguing confluence of spiritual beliefs and practices.

The Vedic religion, documented in the Vedas, the ancient Hindu scriptures, originated in the Indian subcontinent around the same time Zoroastrianism emerged in Persia. Both religions feature deities that personify natural elements and moral concepts, though their roles and significance vary between the faiths.

A striking example of this parallelism is the Zoroastrian *Ahura Mazda* and the Vedic Varuna. Both deities embody cosmic order and truth, embodying similar moral attributes. Yet, in the evolution of both religions, *Ahura Mazda* ascends as the supreme deity in Zoroastrianism, while Varuna's prominence declines in the Vedic pantheon.

Moreover, the Zoroastrian concept of *Spenta Mainyu,* the holy spirit opposing the destructive *Angra Mainyu,* echoes the Vedic dichotomy of *Devas* and *Asuras*. This dualistic framework signifies the eternal conflict between good and evil, a prevalent theme in both religions.

Notably, the word "*Ahura*" in Zoroastrianism and "*Asura*" in Vedic religion, both signifying a class of deities, are linguistically similar, just as the Zoroastrian "*Daeva*" and the Vedic "*Deva*." However, their connotations inverse: *Ahura*s are benevolent in Zoroastrianism, as are *Devas* in Vedic religion, while *Daevas* are malevolent spirits in Zoroastrianism, akin to *Asuras* in the Vedic belief system.

This inversion may hint at an ideological schism between the early Zoroastrian and Vedic communities. Zoroaster's reformist theology, which promoted monotheism and decried the worship of *Daevas,* might have led to this divergence, redefining entities previously revered or reviled.

This study of the shared elements and distinctions between Zoroastrianism and the Vedic religion reveals the dynamic interplay between cultures and faiths. It underscores the fluidity of spiritual beliefs, shaped and reshaped by historical, cultural, and theological shifts. As we venture further in subsequent chapters, we'll continue to unravel Zoroastrianism's complex atlas, marked by enduring principles, evolving interpretations, and cross-cultural influences.

XXI: THREE SONS OF FEREYDUN AND THREE SONS OF NOAH: ECHOES OF A COMMON NARRATIVE

Comparative mythology illuminates the shared narratives that transcend cultural and geographical boundaries. One such narrative that emerges in Zoroastrian and biblical texts is the story of a legendary hero's three sons. In Zoroastrian tradition, this tale is centered around the ancient Iranian king, *Fereydun*, while in the Abrahamic faiths, it revolves around the patriarch, Noah.

Fereydun, a pivotal figure in the *Shahnameh*, the Persian epic of kings, is depicted as a wise and just ruler who triumphs over the tyrannical rule of the evil *Zahhak*. *Fereydun* had three sons: *Salm*, *Tur*, and *Iraj*. After *Fereydun*'s death, his empire was divided among his sons. This division led to conflict and ultimately, the murder of *Iraj* by his envious brothers.

This tale echoes the biblical story of Noah and his sons, Shem, Ham, and Japheth. After surviving the great flood, Noah divided the world among his sons. The biblical narrative also hints at a conflict between Noah's sons, as Ham's disrespectful act towards his father led to a curse on his lineage.

Although the specific narratives differ, the underlying themes of a world divided and ensuing fraternal conflict are strikingly similar. The depiction of three brothers, representative of the divisions of the world, signifies the universal struggle for power and the consequent strife. These narratives underscore the ethical concerns of justice, fraternal duty, and the tragic consequences of greed and envy.

It's important to note that such parallel narratives do not necessarily indicate a direct influence of one tradition on the other. They might instead point towards a shared pool of ancient mythological motifs. These motifs, shaped by universal human experiences and anxieties, might have been expressed through the cultural lens of various civilizations, giving rise to similar narratives in different religious traditions.

By exploring these narrative parallels, we gain a deeper understanding of the human quest for meaning and morality. These shared stories bind us together, illuminating the common threads in our collective spiritual quest, regardless of cultural or religious affiliations. We'll explore more such fascinating facets of Zoroastrianism in the upcoming chapters.

XXII: Pairi-daeza: Paradise and the Enclosed Gardens

An important concept in Zoroastrianism is that of the '*pairi-daeza*,' the Old Persian term that originally referred to a walled or enclosed garden. Over time, the word was incorporated into various languages, taking on new meanings and nuances. It eventually evolved into the term 'paradise,' now widely used in English and many other languages to denote a place of ideal beauty and bliss.

In its original context, *pairi-daeza* referred to an enclosed space, a sanctuary where harmony and balance reigned, reflecting the ideal state of the world as envisioned by *Ahura*

Mazda. It was a symbol of earthly perfection and order, a microcosm that echoed the divine wisdom and harmony of the macrocosm.

Zoroastrian cosmology considers the world as a grand *pairi-daeza*, created by *Ahura Mazda* as an arena for the struggle between good and evil, truth and deceit. This cosmic struggle is reflected on a smaller scale in human actions and decisions. Each act of piety and righteousness, each adherence to the principles of good thoughts, good words, and good deeds, contributes to maintaining the world's harmony, turning it closer to the state of a divine *pairi-daeza*.

Moreover, *pairi-daeza* signifies the promise of an ideal afterlife for the righteous. In Zoroastrian eschatology, individuals who lead virtuous lives are promised a place in the heavenly *pairi-daeza*, a realm of endless peace, joy, and spiritual fulfillment.

This concept of *pairi-daeza* or paradise found its way into other religious traditions, including Christianity and Islam, serving as a universal symbol of divine reward and the aspiration for a world devoid of suffering and discord.

In the following chapters, we'll continue to dive into Zoroastrianism's profound influences, revealing the spiritual wealth it has offered to the atlas of world religions and philosophies. Stay tuned as we navigate the captivating world of *Yazatas, Urvan,* and *Fravashi,* central elements in the understanding of Zoroastrian cosmology and anthropology.

XXIII: YAZATAS: DIVINE BEINGS IN ZOROASTRIANISM

In Zoroastrianism, the term '*Yazata*' refers to a class of divine beings that occupy an important place within the faith. The word '*Yazata*' can be translated as "worthy of worship" or "worthy of reverence," signifying their elevated status and role in the Zoroastrian cosmology.

Yazatas are celestial beings representing various aspects of the natural world and embodying specific qualities or virtues. They serve as intermediaries between humans and the supreme deity, *Ahura Mazda*. These divine beings are viewed as helpers, guardians, and sources of inspiration for individuals in their pursuit of righteousness.

Among the most revered *Yazatas* is *Mithra,* associated with the sun and known as the protector of truth and justice. *Mithra*'s attributes of strength, loyalty, and upholding the cosmic order are highly regarded in Zoroastrian ethics.

Another important *Yazata* is *Anahita,* symbolizing the life-giving waters and associated with fertility, healing, and wisdom. *Anahita* is often depicted as a goddess, representing the nourishing and purifying properties of water.

Other notable *Yazatas* include Sraosha, the *Yazata* of obedience and the embodiment of righteousness, and *Rashnu,* the *Yazata* of justice and the guardian of the cosmic scales.

Each *Yazata* represents a unique divine quality or power, and Zoroastrians invoke their names and seek their blessings for specific purposes. The worship of *Yazatas* involves offering prayers, performing rituals, and making offerings in their honor.

It's important to note that Zoroastrians do not worship these divine beings as independent deities. Instead, they venerate them as emanations of *Ahura Mazda,* acknowledging their roles as agents of *Ahura Mazda*'s divine plan for the world.

The belief in *Yazatas* reflects the complex understanding of the interconnectedness of the natural and spiritual realms in Zoroastrianism. By recognizing and honoring the divine qualities manifest in these celestial beings, Zoroastrians strive to cultivate those virtues in their own lives, aligning themselves with the cosmic order and the teachings of *Ahura Mazda*.

In the upcoming chapters, we will explore the concepts of *Urvan*, the immortal soul, and *Fravashi*, the ancestral guardian spirit, shedding light on the complex anthropology and spirituality of Zoroastrianism.

XXIV: URVAN: THE IMMORTAL SOUL IN ZOROASTRIANISM

Zoroastrianism places a significant emphasis on the concept of the soul, known as '*Urvan*' in the Avestan language. The belief in the immortality of the soul and its journey after death forms a fundamental pillar of Zoroastrian eschatology.

According to Zoroastrian teachings, each individual possesses an *Urvan*, which is the divine essence that distinguishes humans from other creations. The *Urvan* is viewed as a spiritual entity, distinct from the physical body, and is believed to continue its existence after death.

At the time of death, the *Urvan* begin a journey, transitioning to the spiritual realm. The path it follows is determined by the thoughts, words, and deeds of the individual during their earthly life. Zoroastrianism places great emphasis on personal responsibility, as the *Urvan* is judged based on the choices made during its earthly existence.

If the individual has led a righteous life, adhering to the principles of good thoughts, good words, and good deeds, the *Urvan* progresses towards a state of bliss and union with *Ahura Mazda*. However, if the individual has chosen a path of wickedness and has strayed from the path of righteousness, the *Urvan* faces consequences and experiences a state of torment.

This belief in the immortality of the soul and its accountability for one's actions resonates with the broader understanding of ethics and morality in Zoroastrianism. It serves as a reminder of the importance of leading a virtuous life and the consequences of one's choices in shaping the eternal destiny of the soul.

Zoroastrians also believe in the potential for the soul to undergo a process of purification after death. Through prayers, rituals, and the remembrance of the divine, the living can aid the departed soul in its journey towards spiritual enlightenment and eventual union with *Ahura Mazda*.

The concept of *Urvan* further highlights the interconnectedness of the human and divine realms in Zoroastrian thought. It emphasizes the eternal nature of the soul and the ultimate goal of aligning one's individual will with the divine will, thus attaining spiritual perfection.

In the following chapter, we will explore another essential concept in Zoroastrianism: *Fravashi*, the ancestral guardian spirit. This concept holds deep significance in understanding the bond between the living and their ancestors, as well as the spiritual guidance and protection provided by these ancestral spirits.

XXV: FRAVASHI: ANCESTRAL GUARDIAN SPIRITS IN ZOROASTRIANISM

Fravashi is a central concept in Zoroastrianism that pertains to the ancestral guardian spirits. These spirits are believed to be the divine essence of the departed souls of righteous individuals who have passed away.

The term "*Fravashi*" derives from the Avestan word "*fravardigan*," which means "to choose" or "to select." The *Fravashis* are considered as the chosen ones, embodying the accumulated wisdom, blessings, and protection of the righteous ancestors.

In Zoroastrian belief, each person has their own *Fravashi,* which acts as a spiritual guide and protector throughout their life. The *Fravashi* is believed to have existed even before the individual's birth and remains connected to them throughout their earthly journey.

The *Fravashis* not only provide spiritual support and guidance to the living but also serve as a bridge between the human and divine realms. They intercede on behalf of the living, offering prayers and blessings to *Ahura Mazda* and other divine beings. In return, they receive divine assistance and protection for their earthly descendants.

Zoroastrians hold the *Fravashis* in high regard and honor them through various rituals and ceremonies. One such significant occasion is the *Fravardigan* festival, which is celebrated annually to commemorate and honor the *Fravashis* of departed ancestors. During this festival, families gather at the gravesites of their loved ones, offering prayers, reciting sacred verses, and making offerings of food, flowers, and other symbolic items.

The belief in *Fravashis* highlights the importance of ancestral connections and the intergenerational bonds within the Zoroastrian community. It underscores the understanding that the actions and choices of one's ancestors continue to shape and influence the lives of their descendants.

Furthermore, the *Fravashis* represent the collective soul of the community, serving as a unifying force and a source of strength and inspiration. They symbolize the spiritual lineage and heritage of the Zoroastrian people, fostering a sense of belonging and continuity across generations.

In addition to honoring individual *Fravashis,* Zoroastrians also venerate the *Fravashis* of great spiritual figures and historical heroes. These *Fravashis,* known as the *Fravashis* of the righteous, are regarded as powerful celestial beings who intercede on behalf of the community as a whole. They are invoked in prayers and rituals, seeking their blessings, protection, and guidance for the entire Zoroastrian community.

The belief in *Fravashis* extends beyond the human realm. It encompasses all living creatures and even the natural elements. Zoroastrians view the *Fravashis* as universal spirits, embodying the divine essence present in all of creation. This understanding reinforces the interconnectedness of all beings and the shared responsibility of stewardship and care for the environment.

The concept of *Fravashi* reflects the Zoroastrian belief in the continuity of life and the enduring influence of righteous ancestors. It affirms the belief that the actions and values of the past continue to shape and guide the present and future generations.

As we continue our study of Zoroastrianism, we will dive into the complex rituals and practices associated with priesthood and the various roles within the Zoroastrian religious hierarchy. We will examine the responsibilities and significance of *Osta, Osti, Ervad* (*Hirbod*), *Mobed,* and *Dastur,* shedding light on the organizational structure and the vital role played by these individuals in preserving and propagating the Zoroastrian faith.

XXVI: THE ZOROASTRIAN PRIESTHOOD: GUARDIANS OF RITUAL AND SPIRITUAL KNOWLEDGE

The Zoroastrian priesthood holds a crucial role in the preservation and propagation of the Zoroastrian faith. Comprised of various ranks and titles, the priesthood encompasses individuals with distinct responsibilities, ranging from the *Osta* to the *Dastur*. Each role contributes to the maintenance of religious rituals, the interpretation of sacred texts, and the guidance of the Zoroastrian community.

1. *Osta*: At the foundational level of the priesthood is the *Osta*, a term derived from the Avestan word "*Hvasta*,"

meaning "one who offers libations." The *Osta* plays a vital role in conducting rituals and ceremonies, serving as the intermediary between the divine and human realms. They are responsible for performing the *Yasna,* the central liturgical ritual of Zoroastrianism, which involves the recitation of hymns and prayers.

2. *Osti*: The *Osti* is an assistant to the *Osta,* providing support during rituals and ceremonies. They assist in the preparation of sacred implements, the handling of ritual offerings, and the maintenance of sacred fires. The *Osti*'s duties ensure the smooth flow of rituals and the adherence to prescribed practices.

3. *Ervad* (*Hirbod*): The title of *Ervad,* also known as *Hirbod,* is bestowed upon individuals who have undergone extensive religious education and training. They possess in-depth knowledge of Zoroastrian scriptures, rituals, and the principles of the faith. *Ervads* are entrusted with the responsibility of performing complex ceremonies, including those related to marriage, initiation, and death.

4. *Mobed*: The *Mobed* is a higher rank within the priesthood, denoting a senior religious authority and scholar. *Mobeds* undergo advanced theological training, specializing in the interpretation of Avestan texts and the application of religious laws. They are responsible for guiding the community in

matters of religious doctrine and ethics, resolving disputes, and offering spiritual counsel.

5. *Dastur*: The highest-ranking position within the Zoroastrian priesthood is that of the *Dastur*. *Dasturs* are regarded as the supreme religious authorities and custodians of the faith. They possess extensive knowledge of the *Avesta*, including its rituals, prayers, and philosophical teachings. *Dasturs* provide spiritual leadership, oversee the training and ordination of priests, and serve as guardians of Zoroastrian traditions and heritage.

The Zoroastrian priesthood embodies a rich tradition of knowledge transmission, with education and apprenticeship playing a significant role in the development of religious leaders. Individuals aspiring to become priests undergo rigorous training, studying ancient texts, mastering rituals, and imbibing the ethical principles and values of the faith.

The priesthood's duties extend beyond the spiritual realm, encompassing community leadership and welfare. Priests serve as counselors, mediators, and educators, nurturing the spiritual well-being of the community. They offer guidance on matters of personal conduct, family life, and adherence to ethical standards.

Additionally, priests are responsible for the maintenance and care of the sacred fires, which hold deep significance in Zoroastrian worship. These fires symbolize the presence of *Ahura Mazda* and serve as focal points for prayer and devotion. Priests ensure the perpetual burning of these fires, tending to them with utmost reverence and purity.

The Zoroastrian priesthood also encompasses women who hold positions of religious authority, known as *Mobedyars*. While the priesthood has historically been predominantly male, the inclusion of women as religious leaders signifies the evolving role and recognition of female spiritual leadership within the community.

Furthermore, the Zoroastrian priesthood plays a vital role in the preservation and transmission of the *Avesta,* the sacred scriptures of Zoroastrianism. Priests are custodians of the *Avesta*'s knowledge, ensuring its accurate recitation and interpretation. They maintain the integrity of the texts and ensure their accessibility to future generations.

In the upcoming chapters, we will explore the significance of sacred fires in Zoroastrian worship, the role of *Atar* (fire) and *Aban* (water) in Zoroastrian rituals, and the unique architectural structures known as Towers of Silence. These topics will provide further insights into the practices and beliefs that define Zoroastrianism.

XXVII: SACRED FIRES IN ZOROASTRIANISM: SYMBOLISM AND SIGNIFICANCE

Fire holds a central place in Zoroastrian worship, symbolizing the presence of *Ahura Mazda* and serving as a focal point for devotion and ritual. The maintenance and veneration of sacred fires are vital aspects of Zoroastrian religious practices, representing the interplay between the divine and human realms.

In Zoroastrian belief, fire is regarded as a sacred and purifying element, representing the divine wisdom, light, and warmth bestowed by *Ahura Mazda*. It is considered the earthly representative of the celestial fire, emanating from the spiritual realm. The sacred fires embody the ever-burning flame of devotion and the eternal connection between humans and the divine.

Zoroastrians maintain multiple types of sacred fires, each serving a specific purpose and held in high reverence:

1. *Atash Bahram*: The *Atash Bahram,* meaning "Victorious Fire," is the highest grade of sacred fire in Zoroastrianism. It represents the victorious presence of *Ahura Mazda* and encompasses a collection of sixteen different types of fires. These fires are consecrated through complex rituals and require continuous attendance and maintenance by the priesthood.

2. *Atash Adaran*: The *Atash Adaran,* or "Fire of Adar," is the second-highest grade of sacred fire. It is considered a source of healing and protection, and its maintenance follows strict protocols and rituals. The *Atash Adaran* fire is tended to by the priesthood and is believed to possess spiritual potency and the ability to purify the environment.

3. *Atash Dadgah*: The *Atash Dadgah,* or "Fire of Worship," is a grade of sacred fire maintained in Zoroastrian temples or fire temples. It serves as a place of communal worship, where rituals and prayers are conducted by the priesthood and the community. The *Atash Dadgah* symbolizes the collective devotion and spiritual unity of the Zoroastrian community.

4. *Atash Niyayesh*: The *Atash Niyayesh,* or "Fire of Praise," is a smaller fire maintained in individual homes or prayer rooms. It allows individuals to engage in personal devotion, offering prayers and expressing gratitude to *Ahura Mazda*. The *Atash Niyayesh* represents the individual's connection with the divine, fostering a sense of personal spiritual relationship.

The maintenance and care of these sacred fires are of utmost importance in Zoroastrian worship. Priests, or *Mobeds,* are responsible for the tending of the fires, ensuring their continuous burning, purity, and proper observance of rituals. The sacred fires are fed with fragrant woods, such as sandalwood and frankincense, creating a mesmerizing ambiance of spirituality and reverence.

Zoroastrians believe that the sacred fires act as conduits of spiritual energy and blessings. The fires are seen as channels through which prayers and offerings reach *Ahura Mazda,* and the blessings and divine grace are transmitted back to the worshipper. The fire's purifying qualities are believed to cleanse the devotee of impurities and negative influences, enhancing spiritual connection and growth.

The reverence for fire also extends to the practice of fire rituals, known as '*yasna*' or '*jashan*.' These rituals involve the recitation of sacred hymns, prayers, and the making of ritual offerings. The fires serve as the focal point of these ceremonies, symbolizing the presence of *Ahura Mazda* and the divine energies invoked through the rituals.

It's important to note that Zoroastrians do not worship fire as a deity in itself but venerate it as a sacred symbol of divine presence. Fire represents the divine illumination, wisdom, and transformative power that guide individuals on the path of righteousness and spiritual enlightenment.

In the following chapter, we will explore the significance of water in Zoroastrian rituals and beliefs, highlighting the role of *Aban,* the sacred element associated with purity and rejuvenation.

XXVIII: Aban: The Sacred Element of Water in Zoroastrianism

Water holds profound significance in Zoroastrianism, representing purity, life, and rejuvenation. Known as "*Aban*" in the Avestan language, it is regarded as a sacred element that plays a central role in various Zoroastrian rituals and beliefs.

1. Symbolism of Water: In Zoroastrian thought, water is considered a purifying agent, capable of washing away physical and spiritual impurities. It represents the life-giving force, nourishing and sustaining all living beings. Water is seen

as a vital element that connects humans to the divine and serves as a conduit for spiritual renewal and transformation.

2. Ritual Uses of Water: Water is extensively utilized in Zoroastrian rituals and ceremonies. The ritual of "*Nirang-i-Afargan*" involves the consecration of water through prayers and invocations, imbuing it with divine blessings and spiritual power. This consecrated water, known as "*Nirang*," is then used in various rituals, including the ritual purification of individuals, objects, and spaces.

3. Water as a Source of Healing: Zoroastrianism recognizes the healing properties of water. It is believed to possess the ability to cleanse and restore both physical and spiritual well-being. Water is utilized in rituals of ablution, where individuals wash their hands and face as a symbolic act of purification before engaging in prayer or sacred activities.

4. Water as a Symbol of Renewal: Zoroastrian rituals often involve the pouring or sprinkling of water as a symbolic act of rejuvenation and renewal. This act represents the washing away of impurities and the emergence of a purified state, both physically and spiritually. Water symbolizes the constant flow of life, offering the opportunity for rebirth and transformation.

5. Rituals Involving Water: The "*Jashan*" ceremony is an example of a Zoroastrian ritual that prominently features

water. During this ceremony, water is poured into a sacred vessel, accompanied by prayers and invocations. The water is then shared among the participants, symbolizing the communal sharing of spiritual blessings and divine grace.

6. Natural Bodies of Water: Zoroastrianism also recognizes the sanctity of natural bodies of water, such as rivers, lakes, and springs. These natural water sources are considered sacred, believed to be infused with divine energies and blessings. Pilgrimages to these sacred water bodies are undertaken as acts of devotion, with individuals seeking spiritual purification and connection with the divine.

The reverence for water in Zoroastrianism highlights the interconnectedness of the physical and spiritual realms. It emphasizes the importance of maintaining purity and spiritual cleanliness, both through physical acts of purification and through the cultivation of virtuous thoughts, words, and deeds.

The emphasis on water in Zoroastrian rituals and beliefs echoes the broader recognition of the sanctity of nature within the faith. Zoroastrians view the natural elements as manifestations of *Ahura Mazda*'s divine creation and honor them as channels of divine presence and blessing.

In the subsequent chapter, we will explore the unique architectural structures known as Towers of Silence and their significance in Zoroastrian burial customs. These structures provide insight into the Zoroastrian approach to death, purification, and the relationship between the physical and spiritual realms.

XXIX: TOWERS OF SILENCE: ZOROASTRIAN BURIAL CUSTOMS AND SPIRITUAL TRANSFORMATION

In Zoroastrianism, the Towers of Silence, known as "*Dakhma*" or "*Dokhma*," hold a significant place in the faith's burial customs. These unique architectural structures, found primarily in Iran and India, reflect the Zoroastrian approach to death, purification, and the belief in the transformation of the soul.

1. Purpose of Towers of Silence: The Towers of Silence were designed as open-air structures, situated on elevated locations, away from human settlements. Their primary

purpose was to provide a space for the ritual disposal of the deceased, in accordance with Zoroastrian burial customs.

2. Sky Burial: Zoroastrianism advocates for a form of burial known as "sky burial" or "exposure burial." The deceased are placed atop the Towers of Silence, where they are exposed to the elements and birds of prey, particularly vultures. This method is believed to facilitate the process of purification, allowing the soul to be released from the physical body and ascend to higher spiritual realms.

3. Concept of *Nasu*: Zoroastrianism views the physical body of the deceased as impure and associated with the spiritual state of "*Nasu*." *Nasu* represents the temporary contamination of the body by death. By exposing the body to the elements and the scavenging birds, Zoroastrians believe that the impurity is absorbed, while the soul begins its journey toward spiritual purification.

4. Role of Vultures: Vultures play a crucial role in the Zoroastrian burial practice. Their presence on the Towers of Silence aids in the disposal of the deceased's remains, as they consume the flesh. Zoroastrians consider the vultures to be sacred and performing a vital spiritual duty, as they assist in the process of purification and the release of the soul.

5. Environmental Considerations: In recent years, the tradition of sky burial has faced challenges due to declining

vulture populations and concerns about environmental impact. As a result, alternative methods of burial, such as using solar reflectors or underground chambers, have been adopted by some Zoroastrian communities while still maintaining the core principles of purification and separation of the body from the elements.

6. Rituals and Ceremonies: Before the body is placed on the Towers of Silence, specific rituals and prayers are performed by the priesthood and family members. These rituals are aimed at ensuring a respectful and dignified passage for the deceased and invoking divine blessings for the soul's journey. The ceremonies reaffirm the Zoroastrian belief in the soul's transition and spiritual transformation.

The practice of sky burial and the use of Towers of Silence highlight the Zoroastrian emphasis on the duality of physical and spiritual realms, as well as the belief in the soul's eventual liberation from the constraints of the material world.

It's important to note that the Zoroastrian approach to death and burial customs may vary among different communities and regions. While the core principles remain consistent, cultural adaptations and local circumstances have led to certain variations in the rituals and practices associated with burial.

In the subsequent chapter, we will explore the *Council of Tehran Mobeds* and its role in the preservation and governance of Zoroastrian religious affairs. This governing body plays a crucial role in maintaining the unity and cohesion of the Zoroastrian community, as well as safeguarding the religious traditions and practices.

XXX: COUNCIL OF TEHRAN MOBEDS: GUARDIANS OF ZOROASTRIAN RELIGIOUS AFFAIRS

The *Council of Tehran Mobeds,* also known as the *Anjuman-e-Mobedan,* is an important governing body in Zoroastrianism. Based in Tehran, Iran, it serves as a central authority for the Zoroastrian community, overseeing religious affairs, preserving traditions, and fostering unity among Zoroastrians.

1. Establishment and Structure: The *Council of Tehran Mobeds* was established in the early 20th century, during a period of revitalization and organization within the Zoroastrian

community. It was formed to address the need for a centralized institution that could provide guidance and governance in religious matters. The *Council* consists of elected representatives from the Zoroastrian priesthood, known as *Mobeds,* who hold various responsibilities within the community.

2. Preservation of Religious Traditions: The *Council of Tehran Mobeds* plays a crucial role in the preservation and transmission of Zoroastrian religious practices and rituals. It ensures the adherence to traditional customs and ceremonies, overseeing the training and ordination of *Mobeds,* and promoting the correct performance of sacred rituals. The *Council* works to maintain the authenticity and integrity of Zoroastrian traditions in the face of modern challenges.

3. Spiritual Guidance: As a governing body, the *Council* provides spiritual guidance to the Zoroastrian community. It serves as a resource for religious knowledge, addressing queries related to religious practices, ethics, and interpretation of Zoroastrian scriptures. The *Council's* *Mobeds* offer counsel and support to individuals seeking guidance in matters of faith, personal conduct, and family life.

4. Community Welfare: The *Council of Tehran Mobeds* is also responsible for addressing the welfare and well-being of the Zoroastrian community. It oversees the administration of religious institutions, such as fire temples and community cen-

ters, ensuring their proper functioning and maintenance. The *Council* also works to address social, educational, and cultural needs within the community, fostering a sense of unity and solidarity.

5. Interfaith Dialogue: The *Council* actively engages in interfaith dialogue, promoting understanding and cooperation between different religious communities. It seeks to foster mutual respect and tolerance, promoting peaceful coexistence and collaboration among diverse religious groups. The *Council*'s involvement in interfaith initiatives contributes to the broader efforts of promoting harmony and respect among different faith traditions.

6. Advocacy and Representation: The *Council of Tehran Mobeds* represents the Zoroastrian community in matters of public policy and government affairs. It advocates for the rights and interests of Zoroastrians, ensuring their inclusion and recognition within broader society. The *Council* works to raise awareness about the Zoroastrian faith, its teachings, and contributions to the cultural and religious heritage of Iran.

The *Council of Tehran Mobeds* serves as a unifying force within the Zoroastrian community, promoting the values of unity, integrity, and adherence to religious principles. Through its governance, preservation of traditions, and advocacy efforts, it upholds the rich heritage of Zoroastrianism and supports the spiritual well-being of its followers.

In conclusion, the journey through the various chapters of this book has offered a comprehensive study of Zoroastrianism's esoteric teachings and the significance of the priesthood of the fire. From the foundational teachings of Zoroaster to the intricacies of *Ahura Mazda, Asha,* and the celestial beings known as *Yazatas,* we have dived into the depths of this ancient faith. We have discussed the sacred scriptures of the *Avesta,* the rituals and symbolism associated with fire and water, and the customs surrounding death and the afterlife.

Through this journey, we have gained insights into the profound philosophy of Zoroastrianism, its ethical teachings, and its emphasis on the eternal struggle between good and evil. We have explored the roles and responsibilities of the Zoroastrian priesthood, from the *Osta* and *Osti* to the *Dastur,* in preserving the rituals, interpreting the scriptures, and guiding the community in matters of faith.

The concepts of *Urvan,* the immortal soul, and *Fravashi,* the ancestral guardian spirit, have shed light on the complex anthropology and spirituality of Zoroastrianism. We have witnessed the interconnectedness of the natural and spiritual realms, the importance of personal responsibility, and the belief in the ultimate triumph of good over evil.

From the *Fire Temple of Yazd* to the Towers of Silence, we have explored the physical manifestations of Zoroastrian worship and burial customs, symbolizing the spiritual journey of the soul and the purification of the earthly remains. We have recognized the sacredness of fire and water, the rituals that involve them, and the transformative power they represent.

We have discussed the *Council of Tehran Mobeds* and its crucial role in preserving religious traditions, providing spiritual guidance, and fostering unity within the Zoroastrian community. The *Council*'s efforts to maintain the authenticity of Zoroastrian practices, promote interfaith dialogue, and advocate for the community's welfare reflect its commitment to the principles and values of the faith.

Zoroastrianism, with its developed atlas of teachings and practices, continues to inspirit and mystify believers and scholars alike. Its mystical and esoteric nature invites individuals to go on a spiritual pathway, seeking enlightenment, wisdom, and a deeper understanding of the eternal truths it espouses.

As we conclude this study, let us reflect upon the enduring legacy of Zoroastrianism and the profound impact it has had on the religious, philosophical, and cultural traditions of the world. May the teachings of Zoroaster keep inspiring and guide those who seek truth, righteousness, and the illumination of the divine flame that burns within us all.

PART 2: ZOROASTRIAN ESCHATOLOGY

I: THE ORIGINS OF ZOROASTRIAN ESCHATOLOGY

Zoroastrianism, one of the world's oldest religions, traces its origins back to the visionary prophet Zarathustra (also known as Zoroaster). Emerging in ancient Persia during the second millennium BCE, Zarathustra's teachings laid the foundation for a profound eschatological belief system that continues to enthrall and inspirit followers to this day. In this chapter, we start on a path to explore the origins of Zoroastrian eschatology, seeking to unravel the rich atlas of beliefs and concepts that shaped this mystical tradition.

To understand the origins of Zoroastrian eschatology, it is essential to examine the historical and cultural context in which Zarathustra lived. Zarathustra was born in a time of great social and religious change in ancient Persia. The region was marked by polytheism, with various deities and cults vying for devotion. Against this backdrop, Zarathustra emerged as a visionary figure, offering a monotheistic perspective centered around the worship of *Ahura Mazda,* the Wise Lord.

According to Zoroastrian tradition, Zarathustra received a divine revelation from *Ahura Mazda,* calling him to spread a message of truth and righteousness. This revelation, encompassing both ethical teachings and esoteric insights, formed the basis of Zoroastrian eschatology. Through his visionary experiences, Zarathustra gained profound insights into the cosmic battle between the forces of good and evil, which became a central theme in Zoroastrian eschatological beliefs.

At the heart of Zoroastrian eschatology lies the concept of a cosmic battle between *Ahura Mazda,* the embodiment of goodness, wisdom, and light, and *Angra Mainyu* (*Ahriman*), the personification of evil, ignorance, and darkness. This dualistic struggle between the opposing forces of good and evil permeates every aspect of Zoroastrian eschatology, shaping the destiny of both the material and spiritual worlds.

Zarathustra's teachings marked a significant shift in the religious landscape of ancient Persia. By introducing the concept of dualism, Zarathustra sought to explain the coexistence of good and evil, order and chaos, within the universe. This dualistic framework profoundly influenced Zoroastrian eschatology, providing a lens through which adherents understood the ultimate fate of the cosmos and human souls.

The *Gathas*, a collection of hymns attributed to Zarathustra, serve as a primary source for understanding the origins of Zoroastrian eschatology. These poetic verses convey Zarathustra's profound insights into the nature of existence, the divine order, and the eschatological destiny of the universe. Through the *Gathas*, Zarathustra emphasized the importance of personal responsibility, ethical conduct, and the quest for spiritual enlightenment in navigating the cosmic battle.

While the *Gathas* provide a foundational understanding of Zoroastrian eschatology, it is crucial to recognize the subsequent developments and elaborations that shaped this belief system over time. The *Avesta*, the primary sacred text of Zoroastrianism, contains a wealth of eschatological teachings that expound upon the concepts introduced by Zarathustra. These texts include the *Yashts, Vendidad,* and *Visperad,* among others, each shedding light on different aspects of the eschatological framework.

In this chapter, we have gone on a journey to uncover the origins of Zoroastrian eschatology. From the historical and cultural context in which Zarathustra lived to the revelations he received from *Ahura Mazda,* we have begun to unravel the complex web of beliefs that form the foundation of this mystical tradition. The cosmic battle between *Ahura Mazda* and *Angra Mainyu,* the emergence of dualism, and the role of the *Gathas* and subsequent texts have all played pivotal roles in shaping the eschatological landscape of Zoroastrianism. As we carry on our study in the subsequent chapters, we will dive further into the multifaceted nature of *Frashokereti, Kshatra Vairya,* and the coming of *Saoshyant*, unraveling the esoteric wisdom that underpins Zoroastrian eschatology.

II: AHURA MAZDA AND ANGRA MAINYU: THE COSMIC BATTLE

At the heart of Zoroastrian eschatology lies the epic cosmic battle between *Ahura Mazda,* the Wise Lord, and *Angra Mainyu* (also known as *Ahriman*), the embodiment of evil. This profound struggle between the forces of light and darkness shapes the destiny of the universe and influences the eschatological beliefs of Zoroastrianism. In this chapter, we dive deeper into the multifaceted nature of this cosmic battle, seeking to unravel its origins, significance, and implications within the framework of Zoroastrian eschatology.

To comprehend the cosmic battle, it is essential to understand the origins and nature of *Ahura Mazda* and *Angra Mainyu*. *Ahura Mazda*, the supreme deity in Zoroastrianism, represents goodness, wisdom, and divine light. *Angra Mainyu*, on the other hand, embodies evil, ignorance, and darkness. These two opposing entities are believed to have existed since the dawn of creation, locked in eternal struggle.

The cosmic battle between *Ahura Mazda* and *Angra Mainyu* is not merely a physical clash but rather a metaphysical and symbolic representation of the struggle between good and evil, order and chaos. It serves as a reflection of the inner conflicts experienced by individuals and the broader cosmic forces that shape the destiny of the world. The battle unfolds on various levels, encompassing the spiritual, moral, and material realms.

The concept of dualism in Zoroastrianism elucidates the existence of opposing forces within the cosmos. *Angra Mainyu*'s presence represents the presence of evil, which challenges the divine order established by *Ahura Mazda*. Zoroastrian eschatology emphasizes the active participation of individuals in aligning themselves with *Ahura Mazda* and combating the influence of *Angra Mainyu*. It underscores the human responsibility to contribute to the triumph of good over evil.

The cosmic battle between *Ahura Mazda* and *Angra Mainyu* extends to the realm of creation itself. According to Zoroastrian beliefs, *Angra Mainyu* seeks to corrupt and destroy the material world, leading to disorder and chaos. *Ahura Mazda,* on the other hand, is the ultimate creator who strives to maintain the cosmic order and preserve the harmony of existence. The battle manifests in the perpetual conflict between creation and destruction, renewal and decay.

Zoroastrian eschatology acknowledges the pivotal role of humans in the cosmic battle. Human beings are viewed as active participants, granted free will to choose between aligning themselves with the forces of good or succumbing to the influence of evil. Through ethical choices and righteous actions, individuals can contribute to the victory of *Ahura Mazda* and the eventual triumph of goodness over evil. The battle for the souls of humanity is intertwined with the broader cosmic struggle.

The cosmic battle between *Ahura Mazda* and *Angra Mainyu* has profound eschatological implications. It shapes the understanding of the ultimate fate of the universe and the destiny of individual souls. Zoroastrian eschatology envisions a future where *Ahura Mazda*'s power will triumph over the forces of evil, leading to the restoration of cosmic order and the fulfillment of *Frashokereti,* the final renewal of creation.

Zoroastrian rituals and prayers play a significant role in the cosmic battle. They serve as spiritual tools to invoke the assistance of *Ahura Mazda* and his divine entities in the struggle against evil. Through rituals such as *Yasna* and prayers like the Ahuna Vairya, adherents seek divine guidance and protection, aligning themselves with the forces of light and strengthening their resolve in the cosmic battle.

The cosmic battle between *Ahura Mazda* and *Angra Mainyu* lies at the core of Zoroastrian eschatology. It is a profound struggle between the forces of good and evil, order and chaos. Symbolic, metaphysical, and moral in nature, this cosmic battle encompasses the realms of creation, human existence, and the ultimate destiny of the universe. By understanding the origins, symbolism, and eschatological implications of this cosmic battle, we gain deeper insights into the complex web of beliefs that form the foundation of Zoroastrian eschatology. In the subsequent chapters, we will keep exploring the complex concepts of *Frashokereti, Kshatra Vairya,* and the coming of *Saoshyant,* building upon the profound insights gained from understanding the cosmic battle between *Ahura Mazda* and *Angra Mainyu.*

III: THE DUALISTIC NATURE OF ZOROASTRIAN ESCHATOLOGY

Zoroastrianism is renowned for its dualistic worldview, which forms the bedrock of its eschatological beliefs. In this chapter, we dive deep into the dualistic nature of Zoroastrian eschatology, exploring the contrasting principles of good and evil, order and chaos, and their profound implications for the destiny of the universe and human souls. By unraveling the complex atlas of duality, we gain a comprehensive understanding of the eschatological framework that shapes the Zoroastrian worldview.

Dualism in Zoroastrianism emerges from the concept of cosmic conflict between *Ahura Mazda,* the embodiment of goodness, wisdom, and light, and *Angra Mainyu,* the personification of evil, ignorance, and darkness. The existence of these opposing forces sets the stage for a perpetual struggle within the universe, both on a cosmic and individual level.

Zoroastrian dualism extends beyond the cosmic battle to encompass the ethical choices and actions of individuals. It posits that every person is endowed with free will and must actively choose between aligning themselves with the forces of good or succumbing to the influence of evil. This ethical dimension of dualism places a profound responsibility on individuals to contribute to the triumph of good over evil through righteous conduct and moral choices.

Dualism in Zoroastrian eschatology emphasizes the inherent harmony and balance in the universe. *Ahura Mazda* represents the principle of order and goodness, striving to uphold cosmic harmony, while *Angra Mainyu* seeks to disrupt that balance through chaos and evil. The battle between these opposing forces serves as a catalyst for maintaining the delicate equilibrium between creation and destruction, renewal and decay.

Zoroastrian dualism encompasses both the material and spiritual realms. It highlights the inherent struggle between the physical world and the spiritual realm, emphasizing the importance of aligning one's thoughts, words, and actions with the divine order. This dualistic perspective influences Zoroastrian rituals, which seek to bridge the gap between the material and spiritual, fostering harmony and spiritual elevation.

Central to Zoroastrian eschatology is the pursuit of spiritual enlightenment as a means to transcend the limitations of the material world and align oneself with the forces of light. This quest involves cultivating virtues, seeking wisdom, and attaining a higher level of consciousness. By striving for spiritual enlightenment, individuals contribute to the cosmic battle, enabling the triumph of *Ahura Mazda* and the ultimate fulfillment of eschatological prophecies.

Dualism in Zoroastrianism places significant emphasis on purity and pollution. Purity is associated with goodness, truth, and righteousness, while pollution is linked to evil, falsehood, and wickedness. Zoroastrians strive to maintain purity in their thoughts, words, and deeds, as purity is believed to strengthen the forces of good and weaken the influence of evil. Rituals, prayers, and moral conduct play a crucial role in the purification process.

The dualistic nature of Zoroastrian eschatology extends to the eschatological framework itself. It envisions a future where the forces of good will ultimately triumph over evil, leading to the restoration of cosmic order and the fulfillment of *Frashokereti,* the final renewal of creation. This eschatological dualism serves as a source of hope and inspiration, motivating adherents to actively participate in the cosmic battle and contribute to the eventual triumph of *Ahura Mazda.*

The dualistic nature of Zoroastrian eschatology permeates every aspect of its worldview, from the cosmic battle between *Ahura Mazda* and *Angra Mainyu* to the ethical choices and spiritual quests of individuals. It underscores the profound interplay between good and evil, order and chaos, and serves as a framework for understanding the destiny of the universe and the ultimate fulfillment of eschatological prophecies. By comprehending the dualistic nature of Zoroastrian eschatology, we gain deeper insights into the complex atlas of beliefs that shape the Zoroastrian tradition. In the subsequent chapters, we will continue our study of *Frashokereti, Kshatra Vairya,* and the coming of *Saoshyant,* building upon the foundation of dualism to unravel further mysteries of Zoroastrian eschatology.

IV: FRASHOKERETI: THE FINAL RENEWAL OF CREATION

Frashokereti stands as a central concept in Zoroastrian eschatology, representing the final renewal of creation and the ultimate triumph of *Ahura Mazda* over the forces of evil. In this chapter, we dive deep into the profound and complex nature of *Frashokereti,* seeking to unravel its significance, the processes involved, and its eschatological implications within the framework of Zoroastrian beliefs. Through a comprehensive study of ancient texts and philosophical treatises, we begin our exploration to understand the grand finale of the cosmic drama and the cosmic rejuvenation that awaits.

Frashokereti, meaning "making wonderful," represents the ultimate fulfillment of Zoroastrian eschatology, wherein the world is restored to its original perfection and harmony. It symbolizes the triumph of good over evil, the renewal of creation, and the emergence of a new age characterized by righteousness, truth, and immortality. *Frashokereti* is not merely a physical event but a profound spiritual and metaphysical transformation that engulfs all aspects of existence.

Saoshyant, the savior figure in Zoroastrianism, plays a pivotal role in the process of *Frashokereti. Saoshyant* is believed to be a future messianic figure who will appear at the end of time to restore the world and lead humanity towards salvation. *Saoshyant* embodies the divine wisdom and righteousness necessary to guide humanity through the tumultuous events of the final days and facilitate the coming of *Frashokereti.*

Frashokereti involves a comprehensive purification process, both at the individual and cosmic levels. It necessitates the elimination of evil, falsehood, and impurity from the world, paving the way for the restoration of the divine order. This purification process entails the judgment of souls, the redemption of the righteous, and the punishment of the wicked. Through this process, the cosmic balance is restored, and the world is prepared for its ultimate renewal.

Central to the concept of *Frashokereti* is the resurrection of the dead, wherein the souls of all deceased individuals are brought back to life. This resurrection is not merely a physical event but a spiritual awakening, wherein individuals are reunited with their bodies and face the consequences of their deeds in life. The resurrection serves as a means of accountability, justice, and final redemption, aligning with the cosmic order and paving the way for the renewed creation.

Frashokereti encompasses the renewal of the material world, wherein the physical realm is transformed to reflect the divine perfection. The world is rejuvenated, purified, and restored to its original state, free from the corruption and decay brought forth by evil. Nature flourishes, harmony prevails, and the physical realm becomes a reflection of the divine order. This renewal is not a mere continuation but a complete transformation, bringing forth a new age of righteousness and bliss.

Frashokereti culminates in the establishment of eternal harmony and perfection. The forces of good triumph over evil, and the universe attains a state of everlasting order and righteousness. The struggle between *Ahura Mazda* and *Angra Mainyu* reaches its final resolution, with *Ahura Mazda*'s divine wisdom and righteousness prevailing. In this state of eternal harmony, humanity, nature, and the divine unite in a perpetual state of bliss and enlightenment.

Frashokereti represents the culmination of Zoroastrian eschatology, signifying the final renewal of creation and the ultimate triumph of *Ahura Mazda* over the forces of evil. It encompasses a comprehensive purification process, the resurrection of the dead, and the establishment of eternal harmony. Through the concept of *Frashokereti,* Zoroastrianism provides a vision of hope, justice, and redemption, inspiring adherents to strive for righteousness and contribute to the fulfillment of divine perfection. As we continue our study in the subsequent chapters, we will further unravel the eschatological intricacies surrounding *Kshatra Vairya* and the coming of *Saoshyant,* building upon the foundation laid by *Frashokereti.*

V: Saoshyant: The Savior of the World

Saoshyant, a prominent figure in Zoroastrian eschatology, holds a significant role as the savior who will emerge at the end of time. In this chapter, we dive deep into the concept of *Saoshyant,* exploring the origins, attributes, and eschatological implications associated with this messianic figure in the framework of Zoroastrian beliefs. By unraveling the multifaceted nature of *Saoshyant,* we seek to gain a comprehensive understanding of the role this savior plays in the cosmic drama of Zoroastrian eschatology.

The concept of *Saoshyant* finds its roots in the ancient prophecies of Zoroastrianism. These prophecies, recorded in the sacred texts such as the *Avesta,* foretell the arrival of a future messianic figure who will emerge at the end of time to lead humanity towards salvation and contribute to the final renewal of creation. The prophecies describe the attributes and mission of *Saoshyant,* offering a glimpse into the significance of this figure in Zoroastrian eschatology.

Saoshyant is depicted as a divinely inspired and righteous individual endowed with exceptional wisdom and charisma. The attributes of *Saoshyant* include profound knowledge of the divine truths, the ability to perform miracles, and a deep connection with *Ahura Mazda,* the Wise Lord. *Saoshyant* embodies the divine virtues and serves as a guide and role model for humanity, leading them on the path of righteousness and salvation.

Saoshyant's mission revolves around the restoration of order, justice, and righteousness in the world. This savior figure stands as a beacon of hope and a catalyst for the ultimate triumph of *Ahura Mazda* over the forces of evil. *Saoshyant* is tasked with leading humanity through the final stages of the cosmic battle, facilitating the purification process, and preparing the world for the arrival of *Frashokereti,* the final renewal of creation.

Saoshyant plays a pivotal role in the judgment of souls, a crucial aspect of Zoroastrian eschatology. As the savior figure, *Saoshyant* assists in the evaluation of human deeds, determining the fate of individuals based on their thoughts, words, and actions. The judgment process, overseen by *Saoshyant*, ensures that justice is served, and each individual is held accountable for their choices and contributions to the cosmic battle.

Saoshyant imparts divine wisdom and ethical teachings to humanity, guiding them towards righteousness and enlightenment. The teachings of *Saoshyant* emphasize the importance of truth, compassion, justice, and the pursuit of spiritual growth. *Saoshyant*'s words and actions serve as a source of inspiration and guidance for individuals seeking salvation and striving to align themselves with the forces of good.

Saoshyant shares a profound connection with *Ahura Mazda*, representing the divine channel through which the Wise Lord's will is manifested. *Saoshyant* acts as a mediator between humanity and the divine, facilitating the communication and fostering a deeper understanding of *Ahura Mazda*'s teachings. The connection with *Ahura Mazda* empowers *Saoshyant* with the divine authority necessary to fulfill their mission as the savior of the world.

The emergence of *Saoshyant* holds profound eschatological implications for Zoroastrianism. It signifies the nearing of the end times, the final stages of the cosmic battle, and the impending fulfillment of divine prophecies. The appearance of *Saoshyant* brings hope, salvation, and the promise of a renewed world characterized by righteousness, truth, and harmony. *Saoshyant*'s presence serves as a beacon of light, motivating individuals to actively participate in the cosmic battle and contribute to the ultimate triumph of good over evil.

Saoshyant stands as the savior figure in Zoroastrian eschatology, embodying divine wisdom, righteousness, and compassion. This messianic figure plays a pivotal role in leading humanity towards salvation and contributing to the final renewal of creation. The attributes, mission, teachings, and connection with *Ahura Mazda* make *Saoshyant* an integral part of the cosmic drama that unfolds in Zoroastrian eschatology. As we continue our study in the subsequent chapters, we will further unravel the eschatological intricacies surrounding *Kshatra Vairya* and gain deeper insights into the interplay between these profound concepts within the Zoroastrian worldview.

VI: KSHATRA VAIRYA: THE DOMINION OF RIGHTEOUSNESS

Kshatra Vairya holds a significant place in Zoroastrian eschatology as the concept representing the dominion of righteousness. In this chapter, we dive deep into the multifaceted nature of *Kshatra Vairya,* exploring its origins, attributes, and eschatological implications within the framework of Zoroastrian beliefs. By unraveling the profound meaning of *Kshatra Vairya,* we seek to gain a comprehensive understanding of its role in the cosmic drama of Zoroastrian eschatology.

Kshatra Vairya, often translated as "Desirable Dominion" or "Divine Kingdom," represents the establishment of a righteous and just order in the world. It embodies the dominion of *Ahura Mazda,* the Wise Lord, over the forces of evil, bringing forth an era characterized by righteousness, truth, and harmony. *Kshatra Vairya* stands as the fulfillment of the divine plan, wherein the principles of good prevail over those of evil.

The concept of *Kshatra Vairya* finds its roots in the ancient Avestan texts of Zoroastrianism, particularly in the *Gathas,* hymns attributed to the prophet Zarathustra. The *Gathas* emphasize the establishment of a just dominion based on righteousness and the struggle against evil. Over time, *Kshatra Vairya* evolved into a broader eschatological concept, representing the culmination of the cosmic battle and the triumph of good over evil.

Kshatra Vairya embodies divine attributes, representing the dominion of *Ahura Mazda* over the forces of evil. It is associated with righteousness, justice, wisdom, and divine power. *Kshatra Vairya* ensures the establishment of a just social order, where truth prevails, and the well-being of all creation is upheld. It signifies the divine authority through which *Ahura Mazda* governs the world, guiding humanity towards righteousness and ensuring cosmic harmony.

While *Kshatra Vairya* represents the dominion of *Ahura Mazda,* it also highlights the role of humankind in upholding righteousness and contributing to the establishment of a just order. Zoroastrianism emphasizes the active participation of individuals in the cosmic battle, calling upon them to align themselves with the forces of good, resist evil, and work towards the betterment of society. Through their thoughts, words, and actions, individuals play an integral role in the manifestation of *Kshatra Vairya*.

Kshatra Vairya has profound ethical implications in Zoroastrian eschatology. It underscores the importance of living a righteous life, upholding moral values, and promoting justice and fairness in all aspects of existence. Zoroastrians are called to engage in righteous conduct, cultivate virtues, and contribute to the establishment of a just social order. *Kshatra Vairya* serves as a guiding principle, inspiring individuals to strive for righteousness and align themselves with the divine plan.

Kshatra Vairya is intimately connected to the concept of *Frashokereti*, the final renewal of creation. While *Frashokereti* represents the ultimate fulfillment of divine perfection, *Kshatra Vairya* represents the dominion of righteousness within this renewed creation. *Kshatra Vairya* ensures that the restored world operates under the governance of *Ahura Mazda*, with justice and righteousness prevailing in all realms of existence.

The establishment of *Kshatra Vairya* contributes to the realization of *Frashokereti*.

Kshatra Vairya signifies the ultimate triumph of righteousness and the subjugation of evil. It represents the culmination of the cosmic battle, where *Ahura Mazda*'s dominion is fully established, and the forces of darkness are subdued. This triumph ensures that the divine order prevails, cosmic harmony is restored, and the universe operates according to the principles of righteousness, truth, and justice.

Kshatra Vairya, the dominion of righteousness, holds a profound place in Zoroastrian eschatology. It signifies the establishment of a just order, guided by the principles of *Ahura Mazda*. The attributes, ethical implications, and relationship with *Frashokereti* highlight the significance of *Kshatra Vairya* within the cosmic drama of Zoroastrian beliefs. As we continue our study in the subsequent chapters, we will further unravel the eschatological intricacies surrounding the concept of *Saoshyant* and gain deeper insights into the interplay between these profound concepts within the Zoroastrian worldview.

VII: THE ROLE OF HUMAN ACTIONS IN ESCHATOLOGY

Zoroastrian eschatology emphasizes the profound role of human actions in shaping the destiny of the world and the individual soul. In this chapter, we dive deep into the concept of the role of human actions in eschatology within the framework of Zoroastrian beliefs. By exploring the complex interplay between human agency and the cosmic battle between good and evil, we seek to gain a comprehensive understanding of how individual choices and deeds contribute to the ultimate fulfillment of Zoroastrian eschatological prophecies.

At the core of Zoroastrian ethics lies the principle of *Asha*, which encompasses righteousness, truth, and cosmic order. Human actions are believed to have a direct impact on the preservation or disruption of *Asha* in the world. Through their choices and deeds, individuals either align themselves with the forces of good, thereby upholding *Asha*, or contribute to the influence of evil, causing a disruption in the cosmic balance.

Zoroastrian eschatology acknowledges the existence of free will, granting individuals the ability to choose between good and evil. This free will comes with a profound moral responsibility to exercise one's agency in alignment with the divine order. Each individual is accountable for their choices and actions, with the consequences reverberating in both the material and spiritual realms.

Zoroastrianism places great emphasis on ethical conduct as a means to participate in the cosmic battle between good and evil. Righteous actions, such as honesty, kindness, and justice, contribute to the triumph of good and the preservation of cosmic order. Ethical conduct is seen as a powerful tool through which individuals can actively engage in the eschatological journey and play a part in the ultimate fulfillment of Zoroastrian prophecies.

The concept of karma, known as *Daena* in Zoroastrianism, reflects the notion that every action has consequences.

Zoroastrian eschatology emphasizes that individuals are accountable for their deeds, as these actions shape their spiritual journey and determine their fate in the afterlife. Positive actions generate positive consequences, leading to spiritual growth and closer alignment with *Ahura Mazda*, while negative actions result in negative consequences and distance from divine harmony.

Zoroastrian eschatology includes the judgment of souls, wherein the deeds of individuals are evaluated to determine their ultimate fate. The *Chinvat Bridge*, a symbolic bridge, is believed to be the place of judgment. The righteous, who have upheld *Asha* and acted in accordance with ethical principles, are guided safely across the bridge to eternal bliss. The wicked, however, face the consequences of their actions and may encounter challenges in crossing the bridge.

Zoroastrian eschatology encourages individuals to actively pursue spiritual growth through virtuous conduct, prayer, and devotion. Spiritual growth is seen as a means to align oneself with the forces of good, deepening one's connection with *Ahura Mazda*, and contributing to the cosmic battle. By nurturing the divine spark within and striving for righteousness, individuals enhance their spiritual journey and play an active role in the unfolding eschatological events.

Zoroastrianism emphasizes the possibility of repentance and redemption, even for those who have strayed from the path of righteousness. Through sincere remorse, a genuine desire for spiritual transformation, and active efforts to correct past wrongs, individuals can seek redemption and realign themselves with *Asha*. The pursuit of repentance offers an opportunity for individuals to contribute to the cosmic battle and strive towards spiritual growth.

The cumulative impact of human actions in alignment with *Asha* ultimately contributes to the eschatological transformation. Through the collective efforts of individuals upholding righteousness, the forces of good gain strength, leading to the triumph of *Ahura Mazda* and the fulfillment of eschatological prophecies. Human actions serve as catalysts for the restoration of cosmic order, the renewal of creation, and the ultimate fulfillment of divine perfection.

The role of human actions in eschatology within Zoroastrian beliefs is profound and multifaceted. Through free will, moral responsibility, ethical conduct, and the pursuit of spiritual growth, individuals actively participate in the cosmic battle between good and evil. Each choice and action reverberates in the material and spiritual realms, shaping the destiny of the world and the individual soul. As we continue our study in the subsequent chapters, we will further unravel the eschatological intricacies surrounding the concepts of *Saoshyant* and *Kshatra Vairya,* gaining deeper insights into the interplay between human agency and the cosmic drama within Zoroastrian eschatology.

VIII: THE JUDGMENT OF SOULS: CHINVAT BRIDGE

In Zoroastrian eschatology, the judgment of souls plays a significant role in determining the ultimate fate of individuals in the afterlife. Central to this judgment is the *Chinvat Bridge,* a symbolic bridge that serves as a threshold between the material and spiritual realms. In this chapter, we dive deep into the concept of the judgment of souls at the *Chinvat Bridge,* exploring its significance, the criteria for evaluation, and the eschatological implications within the framework of Zoroastrian beliefs.

The *Chinvat Bridge*, also known as the Bridge of Judgment, holds great symbolic importance in Zoroastrian eschatology. It represents the transitional phase between earthly existence and the afterlife, where the deeds of individuals are evaluated. The bridge serves as a threshold, separating the righteous from the wicked, and symbolizes the journey each soul must undertake to reach its ultimate destination.

At the *Chinvat Bridge*, the souls of the deceased are evaluated based on their deeds and alignment with *Asha*, the principle of righteousness. The judgment process involves the scrutiny of thoughts, words, and actions, with the consequences of each evaluated. The evaluation considers the individual's contribution to the cosmic battle, their adherence to ethical principles, and the impact of their choices on themselves and others.

Zoroastrian eschatology depicts the judgment of souls at the *Chinvat Bridge* as a three-fold process. The first judgment evaluates the deeds of individuals during their earthly lives, determining their initial placement on the bridge. The second judgment considers the consequences of those deeds, resulting in either progress towards salvation or the facing of challenges. The final judgment determines the ultimate destiny of the soul, leading to either eternal bliss or punishment.

The evaluation of souls at the *Chinvat Bridge* is guided by the principles of righteousness, truth, and justice. Individuals are judged based on their adherence to *Asha,* their commitment to ethical conduct, and their contributions to the cosmic battle between good and evil. The thoughts, words, and actions of individuals are scrutinized, taking into account their intentions, sincerity, and the impact of their choices on the world.

Based on the results of the judgment at the *Chinvat Bridge,* souls are rewarded or punished according to their deeds. The righteous, who have upheld *Asha* and acted in accordance with ethical principles, are guided safely across the bridge, leading to eternal bliss in the spiritual realm. The wicked, however, face consequences for their actions and may encounter challenges in crossing the bridge, leading to punishment and distance from divine harmony.

Saoshyant, the savior figure in Zoroastrianism, is intimately connected to the judgment of souls at the *Chinvat Bridge.* As the divinely appointed guide and mediator, *Saoshyant* assists in the evaluation of souls, providing guidance, support, and intercession for those who seek redemption. *Saoshyant* plays a vital role in ensuring fairness, justice, and mercy in the judgment process, allowing opportunities for repentance and salvation.

Zoroastrian eschatology acknowledges the possibility of repentance and redemption, even for those who have strayed from the path of righteousness. At the *Chinvat Bridge,* individuals are given opportunities to confront their past actions, express remorse, seek forgiveness, and actively work towards spiritual transformation. The pursuit of repentance offers a chance for redemption, realignment with *Asha,* and progression towards salvation.

Once souls have undergone judgment at the *Chinvat Bridge,* their journey continues beyond this symbolic threshold. The righteous proceed towards eternal bliss, entering into the spiritual realm where they reunite with *Ahura Mazda* and experience the rewards of their virtuous deeds. The wicked, however, face the consequences of their actions, experiencing punishment and separation from divine harmony.

The judgment of souls at the *Chinvat Bridge* holds profound eschatological implications in Zoroastrianism. It underscores the significance of individual choices and actions, highlighting the accountability of each soul for its deeds. The judgment process contributes to the cosmic battle between good and evil, the restoration of cosmic order, and the fulfillment of Zoroastrian eschatological prophecies.

The judgment of souls at the *Chinvat Bridge* serves as a pivotal aspect of Zoroastrian eschatology, determining the ultimate fate of individuals in the afterlife. Symbolic in nature, this process evaluates the thoughts, words, and actions of individuals, assessing their adherence to righteousness and their contributions to the cosmic battle. The *Chinvat Bridge* stands as a threshold between the material and spiritual realms, offering opportunities for redemption and progression towards eternal bliss or the consequences of one's deeds. As we continue our study in the subsequent chapters, we will further unravel the eschatological intricacies surrounding the concepts of *Saoshyant* and *Kshatra Vairya,* gaining deeper insights into the interplay between individual judgment and the cosmic drama within Zoroastrian eschatology.

IX: THE REWARDS AND PUNISHMENTS OF THE AFTERLIFE

Zoroastrian eschatology envisions the afterlife as a realm of rewards and punishments, wherein the fate of individuals is determined by their deeds and alignment with righteousness. In this chapter, we dive deep into the concept of the rewards and punishments of the afterlife within the framework of Zoroastrian beliefs. By exploring the eschatological implications of individual actions, we seek to gain a comprehensive understanding of how virtue and vice are rewarded or punished in the spiritual realm.

Zoroastrianism teaches that the righteous, those who have upheld righteousness and contributed to the cosmic battle, are rewarded with eternal bliss in the spiritual realm. This realm is described as a place of joy, harmony, and enlightenment, where individuals are united with *Ahura Mazda*, the Wise Lord. The rewards of the afterlife are not limited to material pleasures but encompass spiritual growth, enlightenment, and the fulfillment of divine purpose.

In contrast to the realm of eternal bliss, Zoroastrian eschatology depicts punishment for those who have aligned themselves with evil and disrupted cosmic order. The nature of punishment is described as a state of separation from divine harmony and the consequences of one's actions. It is not depicted as eternal damnation but as a corrective measure aimed at allowing individuals to recognize and rectify their wrongdoings.

The rewards and punishments of the afterlife are closely tied to the concept of karma, known as *Daena* in Zoroastrianism. Karma reflects the notion that every action has consequences, shaping the destiny of the soul in the afterlife. Positive actions generate positive consequences, leading to spiritual growth and closeness to *Ahura Mazda*, while negative actions result in negative consequences, distancing the individual from divine harmony.

Zoroastrian eschatology depicts a hierarchy of rewards and punishments in the afterlife, reflecting the diverse range of individual deeds and the degree of alignment with righteousness. The rewards and punishments are believed to be proportional to one's actions, with individuals facing consequences that correspond to the quality and impact of their deeds. This hierarchy ensures justice and fairness in the eschatological realm.

The judgment of souls, as discussed in previous chapters, plays a crucial role in determining the rewards and punishments of the afterlife. The *Chinvat Bridge* serves as a symbolic threshold where the evaluation of souls takes place. It is through this judgment process that the righteous are guided towards their rewards, while the wicked face the consequences of their actions. Judgment ensures that each individual is held accountable for their choices and deeds.

Zoroastrian eschatology recognizes the possibility of repentance and redemption, even for those who have committed wrongdoings. The afterlife provides opportunities for individuals to reflect on their actions, express remorse, and seek forgiveness. Through sincere repentance, individuals can strive to rectify their past mistakes, align themselves with righteousness, and work towards the redemption of their souls.

Zoroastrian eschatology includes the concept of a purgatorial state called *Hamistagan,* which serves as a transitional realm for souls undergoing purification. Souls in *Hamistagan* face a period of spiritual reflection and cleansing, allowing them to confront their past actions and seek forgiveness. It is through this purgatorial state that individuals have the opportunity to progress towards salvation and eventual rewards.

Zoroastrian eschatology emphasizes the potential for eternal progression and transformation within the afterlife. While individuals may initially face punishments or challenges, the ultimate goal is their spiritual growth and realignment with righteousness. The afterlife serves as a realm of learning, purification, and personal evolution, allowing souls to transcend their past actions and progress towards higher levels of enlightenment.

The rewards and punishments of the afterlife in Zoroastrian eschatology reflect the consequences of individual actions and alignment with righteousness. The realm of eternal bliss awaits the righteous, offering spiritual growth, enlightenment, and union with *Ahura Mazda*. Punishment, on the other hand, serves as a corrective measure aimed at allowing individuals to recognize and rectify their wrongdoings. Through the eschatological framework of rewards and punishments,

Zoroastrianism emphasizes the accountability of each individual and the potential for redemption and eternal progression. As we continue our study in the subsequent chapters, we will further unravel the eschatological intricacies surrounding the concepts of *Saoshyant* and *Kshatra Vairya,* gaining deeper insights into the interplay between individual actions and the cosmic drama within Zoroastrian eschatology.

X: THE RESURRECTION OF THE DEAD

Central to Zoroastrian eschatology is the concept of the resurrection of the dead, a profound event that holds significant spiritual and metaphysical implications. In this chapter, we dive deep into the concept of the resurrection of the dead within the framework of Zoroastrian beliefs. By exploring the eschatological significance and processes associated with this event, we seek to gain a comprehensive understanding of its role in the cosmic drama of Zoroastrian eschatology.

The resurrection of the dead in Zoroastrianism is not merely a physical event but also a spiritual awakening. It represents the reunion of the soul with the body, allowing individuals to experience the consequences of their actions and participate in the final stages of eschatological events. This awakening serves as a means of accountability, justice, and final redemption, aligning with the cosmic order and paving the way for the renewed creation.

The concept of *Frashokereti*, the final renewal of creation, is intimately connected to the resurrection of the dead. *Frashokereti* involves the rejuvenation and purification of the material world, and the resurrection of the dead is an essential aspect of this process. As the world is restored to its original state of perfection, the souls of all deceased individuals are brought back to life, reuniting with their bodies and facing the consequences of their deeds in life.

The resurrection of the dead is intertwined with the judgment of souls, a crucial aspect of Zoroastrian eschatology. Through the resurrection, individuals are held accountable for their choices, thoughts, words, and actions. The judgment process evaluates the deeds of each individual, determining their fate based on their alignment with righteousness. The resurrection allows the judgment to be completed, ensuring justice and fairness in the eschatological realm.

In the resurrection of the dead, individuals face the consequences of their deeds in life. The righteous are rewarded for their virtuous actions, while the wicked bear the burden of their wrongdoings. This process of consequences serves as a means of justice and divine retribution, ensuring that each individual experiences the effects of their choices and contributes to the overall cosmic balance.

The resurrection of the dead involves the reunification of the soul with the body, resulting in the transformation of the physical form. The resurrected bodies are described as imperishable, free from the limitations and ailments of the mortal world. This transformation reflects the renewed state of the material realm in *Frashokereti*, where the physicality is restored to its original perfection.

Saoshyant, the savior figure in Zoroastrianism, plays a significant role in the resurrection of the dead. It is believed that *Saoshyant* possesses the divine power and authority to facilitate the resurrection process, guiding souls back to their bodies and overseeing the judgment of the resurrected individuals. *Saoshyant*'s presence ensures fairness, justice, and the fulfillment of eschatological prophecies.

The resurrection of the dead serves multiple purposes within Zoroastrian eschatology. It provides an opportunity for individuals to face the consequences of their deeds, enabling the realization of divine justice. The resurrection also allows souls to actively participate in the final stages of the cosmic battle, contributing to the triumph of righteousness and the establishment of a renewed world in *Frashokereti*.

The resurrection of the dead ultimately determines the eternal destiny of each individual soul. The righteous, who have aligned themselves with righteousness and contributed to the cosmic battle, are rewarded with eternal bliss in the spiritual realm. In contrast, the wicked face eternal consequences for their actions, experiencing punishment and separation from divine harmony. The resurrection solidifies the eternal fate of individuals, ensuring that justice and cosmic order prevail.

The resurrection of the dead holds profound eschatological significance within Zoroastrianism. It represents a spiritual awakening, the reunification of the soul with the transformed body, and the facing of consequences for individual deeds. The resurrection is complexly connected to the concepts of *Frashokereti*, the judgment of souls, and the role of *Saoshyant*. As we continue our study in the subsequent chapters, we will further unravel the eschatological intricacies surrounding the concepts of *Saoshyant* and *Kshatra Vairya*, gaining deeper insights into the interplay between these profound concepts within the Zoroastrian worldview.

XI: THE ROLE OF RITUALS AND PRAYERS IN ESCHATOLOGY

Rituals and prayers hold a significant place in Zoroastrian eschatology, providing a means for individuals to actively engage in the cosmic battle between good and evil and contribute to the eschatological journey. In this chapter, we dive deep into the concept of the role of rituals and prayers in eschatology within the framework of Zoroastrian beliefs. By exploring the eschatological significance and functions of these practices, we seek to gain a comprehensive understanding of their role in shaping individual spirituality and participating in the fulfillment of Zoroastrian eschatological prophecies.

Rituals in Zoroastrianism are not mere symbolic acts but are believed to possess inherent spiritual power. They serve as a means of connecting with the divine, aligning oneself with the forces of good, and invoking blessings. Rituals can be performed both individually and collectively, allowing individuals to actively participate in the cosmic battle and contribute to the triumph of righteousness.

One of the central aspects of Zoroastrian rituals is the emphasis on purity and cleansing. Purification rituals, such as the ritual of ablution and the consecration of sacred fires, serve as means of removing spiritual impurities and aligning oneself with the forces of good. These rituals play a crucial role in preparing individuals to engage in eschatological events and ensuring their spiritual readiness for the final stages of the cosmic battle.

Prayers form a vital aspect of Zoroastrian rituals, serving as a means of establishing a connection with the divine forces, particularly with *Ahura Mazda*, the Wise Lord. Prayers express devotion, gratitude, and supplication, and seek guidance, protection, and blessings. Through prayers, individuals align their thoughts, intentions, and words with the divine order, fostering a deeper connection with the spiritual realm and participating in the cosmic battle on a spiritual level.

Zoroastrian rituals and prayers aim to contribute to cosmic harmony, fostering an alignment between the material and spiritual realms. By actively engaging in these practices, individuals seek to bring balance, righteousness, and order to the world, aligning their intentions and actions with the divine plan. Rituals and prayers serve as transformative acts, allowing individuals to transcend their limited selves and participate in the fulfillment of Zoroastrian eschatological prophecies.

Rituals and prayers also play a crucial role in preparing individuals for the afterlife. The emphasis on purity, righteousness, and spiritual connection helps individuals cultivate virtues, align their intentions with *Asha,* and strive for spiritual growth. By engaging in these practices, individuals seek to ensure a favorable judgment at the *Chinvat Bridge,* enhance their spiritual journey, and prepare themselves for the rewards of the afterlife.

Zoroastrian rituals and prayers often include symbolic elements that represent eschatological concepts. For example, the consecration of sacred fires symbolizes the presence of *Ahura Mazda* and serves as a focal point for spiritual connection and purification. The use of sacred chants and hymns in prayers carries deep esoteric meanings, representing the invocation of divine forces and the alignment of the human voice with the celestial realms.

Rituals and prayers in Zoroastrianism serve as a means of sustaining the cosmic order and contributing to the maintenance of *Asha*. Through these practices, individuals actively engage in the cosmic battle, resisting the forces of evil, and upholding righteousness. The collective participation in rituals and prayers reinforces the communal bond, creating a unified front against the disruptive forces and furthering the eschatological journey towards the triumph of good.

Rituals and prayers occupy a central place in Zoroastrian eschatology, providing individuals with the means to actively engage in the cosmic battle, cultivate spirituality, and participate in the fulfillment of eschatological prophecies. These practices serve as transformative acts, aligning individuals with righteousness, connecting them with divine forces, and contributing to the restoration of cosmic harmony. As we continue our study in the subsequent chapters, we will further unravel the eschatological intricacies surrounding the concepts of *Saoshyant* and *Kshatra Vairya*, gaining deeper insights into the interplay between these profound concepts and the role of rituals and prayers within the Zoroastrian worldview.

XII: THE COSMIC BATTLE AND THE TRIUMPH OF GOODNESS

At the heart of Zoroastrian eschatology lies the cosmic battle between the forces of good and evil, symbolizing the eternal struggle for righteousness and the ultimate triumph of goodness. In this chapter, we dive deep into the concept of the cosmic battle and its eschatological implications within the framework of Zoroastrian beliefs. By exploring the dynamics of this eternal conflict, we seek to gain a comprehensive understanding of the significance of the cosmic battle and the ultimate victory of goodness in Zoroastrian eschatology.

Zoroastrian eschatology posits a dualistic worldview, in which the cosmic battle represents the perpetual struggle between *Ahura Mazda*, the Wise Lord of Light, and *Angra Mainyu*, the embodiment of darkness and evil. This dualistic framework underscores the contrasting principles of good and evil and the ongoing conflict between these opposing forces.

Humanity plays an integral role in the cosmic battle. Individuals are regarded as active participants who have the capacity to choose between good and evil through their thoughts, words, and actions. The choices made by each individual have a direct impact on the balance of the cosmic battle, either contributing to the triumph of goodness or fueling the forces of darkness.

Zoroastrian eschatology places great emphasis on righteousness as the guiding principle in the cosmic battle. Righteousness, known as *Asha*, embodies truth, justice, and cosmic order. Upholding righteousness and aligning oneself with the forces of good is paramount to contributing to the ultimate triumph of goodness in the cosmic battle.

Angra Mainyu and the forces of evil seek to disrupt cosmic order and spread chaos, falsehood, and injustice. The forces of evil tempt individuals to deviate from righteousness, enticing them towards immoral actions and thoughts. The struggle against these forces necessitates unwavering commitment to righteousness, as individuals actively resist the influence of evil and work towards the triumph of goodness.

Saoshyant, the savior figure in Zoroastrianism, plays a pivotal role in the cosmic battle. As the embodiment of divine wisdom, righteousness, and compassion, *Saoshyant* serves as a beacon of hope and leads humanity in the struggle against evil. *Saoshyant*'s presence strengthens the forces of goodness and inspires individuals to actively participate in the cosmic battle, ultimately contributing to the triumph of righteousness.

Zoroastrian eschatology is replete with prophecies that foresee the ultimate victory of goodness over evil. These prophecies anticipate the defeat and subjugation of *Angra Mainyu*, the restoration of cosmic order, and the establishment of a renewed world characterized by righteousness, truth, and harmony. The eschatological prophecies serve as a source of inspiration and hope, motivating individuals to persevere in the cosmic battle.

The triumph of goodness in the cosmic battle leads to the transformation of the world. It brings forth an era where righteousness prevails, and the forces of evil are subdued. This transformation, known as *Frashokereti*, represents the final renewal of creation, wherein the world is restored to its original state of perfection and harmony.

The cosmic battle is not solely the responsibility of individuals. It necessitates collective effort and solidarity among individuals who share a commitment to righteousness. The cumulative impact of collective actions and intentions reinforces the forces of goodness, amplifying the potential for the triumph of righteousness in the cosmic battle.

The triumph of goodness in the cosmic battle leads to the restoration of cosmic harmony, wherein the principles of righteousness, truth, and justice govern the universe. Cosmic harmony ensures the well-being of all creation, fosters spiritual growth, and allows individuals to align themselves with divine purpose.

The cosmic battle between the forces of good and evil forms the bedrock of Zoroastrian eschatology. It represents the perpetual struggle for righteousness and the triumph of goodness over evil. Humanity's active participation in this battle, the role of *Saoshyant,* the prophecies of eschatological victory, and the restoration of cosmic harmony are all integral components of this cosmic drama. As we continue our study in the subsequent chapters, we will further unravel the eschatological intricacies surrounding the concepts of *Saoshyant* and *Kshatra Vairya,* gaining deeper insights into the interplay between the cosmic battle and the unfolding of Zoroastrian eschatology.

XIII: THE COSMIC TIME CYCLES AND ESCHATOLOGICAL EVENTS

Zoroastrian eschatology encompasses a profound understanding of cosmic time cycles and their relationship to eschatological events. In this chapter, we dive deep into the concept of the cosmic time cycles and the eschatological events that unfold within them, within the framework of Zoroastrian beliefs. By exploring the interplay between time, prophecy, and the unfolding of eschatological events, we seek to gain a comprehensive understanding of how time cycles shape the Zoroastrian worldview and provide a framework for the fulfillment of eschatological prophecies.

Zoroastrianism acknowledges the existence of cosmic time cycles, which are characterized by the rise and fall of civilizations, the progression of spiritual events, and the evolution of the material world. These time cycles are interconnected and operate within larger cycles, reflecting the cyclical nature of existence and the interplay between cosmic forces.

One of the key concepts in Zoroastrian eschatology is the *Long Count,* a vast time cycle that spans thousands of years. Within the *Long Count,* there are smaller divisions known as *Fravashi Epochs,* each encompassing specific eschatological events and prophecies. These epochs mark significant milestones in the unfolding of Zoroastrian eschatology, representing the progression of time towards the ultimate fulfillment of divine purpose.

The *Fravashi Epochs* are associated with specific prophecies and eschatological events. These prophecies provide insights into the nature of the cosmic battle, the coming of *Saoshyant,* the triumph of goodness, and the restoration of cosmic order. The *Fravashi Epochs* serve as markers of time, guiding believers in their understanding of the unfolding eschatological events and inspiring them to actively participate in the cosmic drama.

Zoroastrian eschatology recognizes the cyclic nature of creation and regeneration. The world undergoes cycles of creation, degeneration, and eventual regeneration. These cycles reflect the eternal struggle between good and evil and provide opportunities for spiritual growth, redemption, and the ultimate fulfillment of eschatological prophecies.

Saoshyant, the savior figure in Zoroastrianism, plays a crucial role within the context of cosmic time cycles. *Saoshyant* is believed to appear at specific points within these cycles to guide humanity towards righteousness, deliverance, and the fulfillment of eschatological prophecies. The presence of *Saoshyant* within the time cycles ensures the continuity of divine guidance and the progression towards the ultimate triumph of goodness.

Eschatological events within Zoroastrianism are complexly linked to cosmic time cycles. These events unfold within specific time frames, aligning with the prophecies and the overarching purpose of cosmic order. The judgment of souls, the resurrection of the dead, the triumph of goodness, and the restoration of the world are all tied to the cosmic time cycles, reflecting the interplay between time, divine plan, and the unfolding eschatological journey.

Zoroastrian eschatology acknowledges that time is not static but continuously evolves and progresses. Each moment contributes to the unfolding of eschatological events and the realization of divine purpose. Believers are called to actively engage with the present moment, recognizing its significance within the larger context of cosmic time cycles and their eschatological implications.

While Zoroastrian eschatology acknowledges the cyclical nature of time, it also recognizes the eternal nature of eschatological time. The eschatological events, the triumph of goodness, and the restoration of cosmic order exist beyond the confines of linear time. They reflect the eternal struggle between good and evil and the timeless victory of righteousness over darkness.

The understanding of cosmic time cycles within Zoroastrian eschatology provides a framework for comprehending the unfolding of eschatological events and the fulfillment of prophecies. The *Fravashi Epochs,* the role of *Saoshyant,* and the continuous evolution of time all contribute to the interplay between time, prophecy, and the cosmic drama. As we continue our study in the subsequent chapters, we will further unravel the eschatological intricacies surrounding the concepts of *Saoshyant* and *Kshatra Vairya,* gaining deeper insights into the interconnection between cosmic time cycles and the eschatological journey within Zoroastrian beliefs.

XIV: THE SIGNS OF THE FINAL JUDGMENT

Zoroastrian eschatology contains a rich atlas of signs and omens that herald the arrival of the final judgment, marking the culmination of the cosmic battle and the fulfillment of eschatological prophecies. In this chapter, we dive deep into the concept of the signs of the final judgment within the framework of Zoroastrian beliefs. By exploring these signs and their eschatological significance, we seek to gain a comprehensive understanding of the anticipation and preparation for the ultimate judgment in Zoroastrian eschatology.

Signs in Zoroastrian eschatology are symbolic manifestations and events that precede the final judgment. These signs serve as indicators of the approaching end of the cosmic battle, reflecting the cosmic order and the divine plan. They provide believers with guidance, warnings, and opportunities for spiritual reflection and preparation for the eschatological events.

The celestial realm plays a significant role in signaling the approach of the final judgment. Celestial signs include celestial alignments, unusual phenomena in the heavens, and the appearance of celestial bodies that signify the culmination of eschatological events. These signs are believed to reflect the celestial harmony and the alignment of cosmic forces in preparation for the final judgment.

Natural signs are observed in the earthly realm, indicating the imminence of the final judgment. These signs may include earthquakes, floods, famines, and other natural disasters that disrupt the established order and highlight the presence of evil forces. Natural signs serve as reminders of the consequences of human actions and the need for realignment with righteousness.

The social and moral fabric of society also provides signs of the approaching final judgment. Degeneration of ethical values, moral decay, widespread corruption, and the prevalence of injustice and oppression are all indicative of the culmination of the cosmic battle. These signs emphasize the urgency for individuals to uphold righteousness and actively participate in the triumph of goodness.

Saoshyant, the savior figure in Zoroastrianism, is intimately connected to the signs of the final judgment. The appearance of *Saoshyant* and the fulfillment of the prophecies associated with this figure serve as definitive signs that the eschatological events are imminent. *Saoshyant*'s presence inspires hope, faith, and a renewed commitment to righteousness, urging individuals to actively prepare for the final judgment.

Zoroastrian eschatology is accompanied by prophetic writings and scriptures that contain detailed descriptions of the signs of the final judgment. These writings serve as sources of guidance, offering insights into the nature of the signs and their eschatological significance. The prophecies within these texts provide believers with a framework for understanding and interpreting the signs, fostering anticipation and spiritual preparation.

The signs of the final judgment call for individual reflection and preparation. Believers are encouraged to examine their lives, thoughts, words, and actions in light of the approaching eschatological events. The signs serve as reminders of the accountability for one's choices and the need for realignment with righteousness. Individual preparation involves introspection, repentance, and active participation in the cosmic battle.

The signs of the final judgment culminate in the ultimate judgment of souls. This judgment evaluates the deeds of individuals, determining their ultimate fate based on their alignment with righteousness. It is the culmination of the cosmic battle, reflecting the triumph of goodness and the restoration of cosmic order. The signs serve as reminders that the time for accountability and judgment is drawing near.

The signs of the final judgment signify not only the culmination of the cosmic battle but also the beginning of an eschatological transformation. The judgment and the subsequent events pave the way for the renewal of creation, the restoration of harmony, and the establishment of a world characterized by righteousness and divine order. The signs prepare individuals for this transformative process, urging them to actively participate in the fulfillment of eschatological prophecies.

The signs of the final judgment in Zoroastrian eschatology are an atlas of celestial, natural, and social manifestations that signify the approaching culmination of the cosmic battle. These signs serve as reminders, warnings, and opportunities for spiritual reflection and preparation. They highlight the interconnectedness of the celestial, earthly, and human realms and provide believers with a framework for understanding and anticipating the ultimate judgment. As we continue our study in the subsequent chapter, we will further unravel the eschatological intricacies surrounding the concept of *Kshatra Vairya,* gaining deeper insights into its role in the cosmic battle and the fulfillment of eschatological prophecies.

XV: THE ETERNAL HARMONY: AHURA MAZDA'S ULTIMATE TRIUMPH

At the heart of Zoroastrian eschatology lies the ultimate triumph of *Ahura Mazda,* the Wise Lord of Light, and the establishment of eternal harmony. In this final chapter, we dive deep into the concept of *Ahura Mazda*'s ultimate triumph within the framework of Zoroastrian beliefs. By exploring the eschatological implications of this triumph and its significance in the cosmic drama, we seek to gain a comprehensive understanding of the ultimate fulfillment of divine purpose and the eternal harmony that ensues.

Ahura Mazda's ultimate triumph is the culmination of the cosmic battle and the fulfillment of Zoroastrian eschatological prophecies. It represents the victory of goodness, truth, and righteousness over evil, falsehood, and darkness. This triumph reflects the restoration of cosmic harmony, the establishment of divine order, and the realization of *Ahura Mazda*'s divine plan for creation.

Ahura Mazda's triumph brings forth the restoration of cosmic harmony, wherein the forces of evil are subdued, and righteousness prevails. It signifies the renewal and purification of the material world, aligning it with the spiritual realm. The restoration of cosmic harmony ensures the balance and interplay between the material and spiritual realms, fostering the spiritual growth and well-being of all creation.

Saoshyant, the savior figure in Zoroastrianism, plays a pivotal role in *Ahura Mazda*'s triumph. *Saoshyant*'s actions, teachings, and leadership inspire and guide humanity towards righteousness, actively participating in the cosmic battle and contributing to the triumph of *Ahura Mazda*. *Saoshyant* serves as a conduit of *Ahura Mazda*'s divine power, facilitating the fulfillment of eschatological prophecies and the establishment of eternal harmony.

Ahura Mazda's triumph involves the renewal and transformation of creation. It signifies the purification and rejuvenation of the material world, restoring it to its original state of perfection. This renewal brings forth a world characterized by beauty, truth, and justice, where all aspects of creation are aligned with the divine order. It represents the fulfillment of the divine purpose and the manifestation of *Ahura Mazda*'s wisdom and goodness.

Ahura Mazda's triumph signifies the ultimate victory of truth and righteousness. It represents the triumph of *Asha*, the principle of cosmic order, over falsehood and chaos. The establishment of eternal harmony ensures that truth prevails over deception and righteousness prevails over evil. *Ahura Mazda*'s triumph reflects the eternal nature of truth and righteousness, ensuring their perpetuity and dominion in the spiritual realm.

Ahura Mazda's triumph is the ultimate fulfillment of divine purpose. It represents the culmination of the cosmic drama, where every aspect of creation, every event, and every choice finds its place in the grand design. The triumph ensures that every individual's actions, thoughts, and words serve a greater purpose, contributing to the overall cosmic harmony and *Ahura Mazda*'s ultimate triumph.

While *Ahura Mazda*'s triumph is a cosmic event, it requires the active participation of individuals. Each individual's commitment to righteousness, alignment with the divine order, and contribution to the cosmic battle plays a significant role in the ultimate triumph of *Ahura Mazda*. It emphasizes the interconnectedness of all beings and the collective responsibility to uphold and propagate goodness.

Ahura Mazda's triumph leads to the establishment of eternal harmony. In this state, all creation is in perfect harmony with *Ahura Mazda*'s divine plan. Truth, righteousness, and justice permeate every aspect of existence, fostering the spiritual growth, enlightenment, and well-being of all beings. The eternal state of harmony ensures the everlasting bliss, union with *Ahura Mazda*, and continued progression towards higher levels of understanding and fulfillment.

Ahura Mazda's ultimate triumph represents the fulfillment of divine purpose, the restoration of cosmic harmony, and the triumph of truth and righteousness. It signifies the renewal of creation, the role of *Saoshyant*, and the eternal state of harmony. As we conclude our study of Zoroastrian eschatology, we gain a comprehensive understanding of the profound concepts, complex interplays, and the spiritual journey towards *Ahura Mazda*'s ultimate triumph. The wisdom and teachings of Zoroastrianism inspire us to align our lives with truth, righteousness, and cosmic harmony, contributing to the eternal triumph of goodness in the world.

Ω

OMEGA

Dear reader of the Esoteric Religious Studies Series, we express our deepest gratitude for departing on this enlightening adventure. Having dived into the realms of esoteric wisdom, may you carry the flame of knowledge within your being. May the insights gained and the revelations experienced guide your path as you traverse the atlas of life. May the wisdom you have acquired permeate every aspect of your existence, nurturing your spirit and inspiring your actions. May you carry on to seek truth, embrace growth, and walk the path of wisdom with grace and compassion. May your life be a testament to the transformative power of esoteric knowledge.

If you have enjoyed the words of this book, please consider leaving a review in the marketplace you found it so that its content can enrich the lives of others.

OTHER BOOKS IN THIS SERIES

1. Hermeticism and Alchemy in Renaissance Europe
2. Gnosticism: Ancient Mystical Traditions, Sects & Texts
3. Zoroastrianism: Esoteric Teachings and the Priesthood of the Fire
4. Sufism: Persian Mystical Path of Islam
5. Daoist Immortality and Internal Alchemy
6. Theurgy and Neoplatonic Mysticism
7. Shamanism in Siberia: Animism and Nature Worship
8. African Traditional Religions and Spirituality
9. Druidism and Celtic Mysticism
10. Indigenous Australian Dreamtime, Songlines and Ancestral Beings
11. Jyotish: Vedic Astrology
12. Hellenistic Mystery Cults: Thessalian Witchcraft & Ancient Greek Magic
13. Kabbalah: Jewish Mystical Tradition
14. Shinto: Japanese Indigenous Religion
15. Native American Spirituality and Vision Quests
16. Mesoamerican Shamanism and Divination
17. Ancient Egyptian Rituals and Symbolism
18. Norse Mythology and Runes
19. Rastafarianism: Spirituality and Social Movement
20. Jainism: Ascetic Practices and Philosophy
21. Romuva: Baltic Paganism, Witchcraft, and Folklore Revival
22. Vodou: Haitian Creole Religion
23. Maori Spirituality and Creation Myths
24. Hawaiian Huna Healing and Spirituality
25. Theosophy: Blending Eastern and Western Esotericism
26. Tibetan Bon: Ancient Shamanistic Tradition
27. Yoruba Religion and Orisha Worship
28. Esoteric Buddhism: Secret Teachings and Rituals
29. Romani Folklore and Mythology
30. Aztec Mythology and Cosmology
31. Bahá'í Faith: Unity of Religions
32. Hittite Religion and Rituals
33. Spiritualism: Communication with the Spirit World
34. Afro-Caribbean Syncretic Religions
35. Tantra: Ritual Practices and Symbolism
36. Armenian Folk Religion and Beliefs
37. Guarani Mythology and Cosmology
38. Esoteric Aspects of Islam: Batiniyya and Hurufism
39. Manichaeism: Dualistic Religion and Philosophy
40. Finnish Shamanism and Folk Magic
41. Ancient Sumerian Religion and Magic
42. Afro-Brazilian Umbanda and Candomblé
43. Tibetan Oracles and Divination Practices
44. Khoisan Spirituality: San Bushmen Traditions
45. Yezidi Religion: Angel Worship and the Sacred Peacock
46. Kalash Religion: Ancient Indo-Aryan Practices
47. Druze Esotericism: Secret Wisdom and Reincarnation
48. Burmese Nat Worship and Spirit Possession
49. Ancient Canaanite Religion: Rituals, Magical Texts and Spells
50. Etruscan Divination and Augury

51. Ainu Shamanism: Spiritual Practices in Northern Japan
52. Circassian Paganism and Ancestral Customs
53. Tengrism: Central Asian Shamanistic Beliefs
54. Mari El Paganism: Volga-Finnic Indigenous Religion
55. Haida Mythology and Totemism: Healing and Spirit Communication
56. Balinese Hindu-Buddhist Syncretism
57. Aramean Religion and Ancient Semitic Cults
58. Khoekhoen Religion: Southern African Indigenous Beliefs
59. Ojibwe Midewiwin: The Grand Medicine Society
60. Afro-Colombian Religions: Palenque and Santeria
61. Sámi Shamanism: Indigenous Spirituality of Northern Europe
62. Ossetian Folk Religion and Mythology
63. Mithraism: Ancient Mystery Cult of the Roman Empire
64. Ainu Bear Festival and Symbolism
65. Ancient Anatolia: Hittites and Luwians, and Lydian Goddess Cults
66. Toda Shamanism: Indigenous People of South India
67. Mesopotamian Magic and Incantations
68. Mande Paganism: West African Traditional Religions
69. Javanese Kejawen: Mystical Teachings and Rituals
70. Thracian Myth and Greco-Roman Orphic and Dionysian Mysteries
71. Maronite Christianity: Esoteric Practices and Traditions
72. Basque Mythology, Folklore, and Witchcraft
73. Gagauz Folk Religion and Rituals
74. Tagalog Mythology: Anito Spirits and Mythical Creatures
75. Hurrian Religion: Ancient Near Eastern Pantheon
76. Buryat Buddhism: Shamanistic Elements in Tibetan Buddhism
77. Selk'nam Cosmology and Ceremonies
78. Baka Pygmy Spirituality: Central African Indigenous Beliefs
79. Kumyk Paganism: Turkic Indigenous Religion
80. Scythian Religion and Warrior Culture
81. Venda Mythology: Sacred Lake and Rainmaker Rituals
82. Onondaga Longhouse Religion: Iroquois Spiritual Practices
83. Ewe-Fon Voodoo: West African Spiritual Practices
84. Manchu Shamanism: Indigenous Spirituality of Northeast Asia
85. Taíno Religion: Indigenous Beliefs of the Caribbean
86. Ancient Moabite Religion: Worship of Chemosh and Ashtaroth
87. Gallo-Roman Religion: Celtic Influence in Roman Gaul
88. Tsimshian Mythology: Stories of Raven and Trickster Figures
89. Manobo Indigenous Spirituality: Mindanao Tribal Beliefs
90. Pawnee Sacred Bundles and Tribal Ceremonies
91. Batak Shamanism: Indigenous Practices of North Sumatra
92. Breton Folklore: Legends and Supernatural Beings
93. Jivaroan Shamanism: Indigenous Traditions of the Amazon Rainforest
94. Alawite Mystical Teachings and Secret Practices
95. Silesian Folk Religion and Folklore
96. Igbo Odinani: Traditional Religion of the Igbo People
97. Rarámuri Shamanism: Indigenous Spirituality of the Tarahumara
98. Kikuyu Traditional Religion: Sacred Sites and Ancestor Worship
99. Ancient Numidian Religion: North African Indigenous Beliefs
100. Lurs Folk Religion and Rituals

A World of Esoteric Thought

Made in the USA
Columbia, SC
09 July 2025

9bd3c705-4593-47a3-a9d7-1326e2224c23R01